100 Hearts

for joy & inspiration

KAREN ABEND

ISBN 978-1-7345658

Why hearts?

100 Hearts is a compilation of illustrations that explores one of the most widely used and beloved symbols of all time - the heart. Part of the heart symbol's appeal surely lies in its simplicity. In fact, it is so simple that everyone can recognize it and anyone can draw it, no matter how young or old they might be, or how creatively inclined or not they might feel. Its simplicity, though, is deceiving, since what the heart symbol represents is actually quite complex. Not only does it stand for our most vital, life-giving organ, it also signifies the most powerful feeling in our emotional landscape – love. But more than just love, the heart is also our center, the place inside that connects us to who we really are and how we really feel. In other words, the heart symbol is simple in form, but profound in meaning.

Using this concept of the heart symbol as a creative launch pad, the illustrations in this book are playful responses to 100 different human emotions and ways of being in the world. They attempt to express each feeling, each way of being, no matter how complex, in the simplest visual language possible, inspired by the heart symbol itself.

Some days we feel on top of the world. Other days we might not be at our best. But no matter how we are doing or being on any given day, our feelings can be expressed through the lens of our compassionate, loving, and wise hearts. Our feelings are part of the human experience and by affirming them both visually and with words, we can simplify them and attempt to see them for what they really are. With a playful spirit, that is what these illustrations wish to capture, and it is my heartfelt hope that they bring a smile to your face and a lightness to your heart.

The 100 Hearts Journey

100 Hearts is also a journey about learning how to establish a creative practice and experiencing the benefits of that practice over 100 consecutive days of consistent creativity.

The benefits of practice for developing skills in any area are of life are well known, whether it be with sports, cooking, learning an instrument or even driving a car. The more you repeatedly exercise the activity, the easier and more fluid it becomes. Creative skills are no different. For anyone wanting to develop as an artist, no matter the end goal, learning to establish a creative practice in your life can, over time, lead to real transformation and growth.

Starting and maintaining a creative practice seems so straightforward. If you want to be a painter, paint something every day. If you want to be an illustrator, draw something every day. If you want to be a designer, make a new design every day. In my own attempts to establish a creative practice, I learned that it is much harder to do than it seems. A practice is not only about creating something every day, which already feels like a big challenge, but it's also about establishing a routine and having the right mindset, both of which require their own set of skills to master.

With the help of Sketchbook Revival, an online community and support group I founded in 2018, I learned how to master those skills and put them into practice. 100 Hearts is my first successful attempt at applying the Sketchbook Revival experience to a creative practice. Sketchbook Revival serves to connect the experts – the artists with the experience and know-how of keeping up a successful creative practice – with creativity lovers from around the globe who seek inspiration, guidance and community to help them sustain a long-term commitment to their passion. It's a two-part mission: creative exploration to discover the myriad approaches, techniques and styles available to us; and maintaining consistency by committing to a regular creative practice that is the key for a thriving creative life.

The 100 Hearts series of images shared in this book is just one example of what's possible when exploring the power of practice using the same motif, techniques and approach every day for 100 days. Each image builds on the last, offering a new opportunity to practice skills with color, composition, imagination, symbolism, technique and style. With repeated practice, the skills will develop, shift and evolve. Together, the hearts affirm that no matter how seemingly simple or quick a practice may be, over time the benefits of the consistent commitment will add up to something more. They affirm that what's important is to have fun, play, enjoy the process and be curious. Finally, for anyone who is struggling with their own practice or wishes they could be more creative, it is my sincere hope that 100 Hearts affirms that if I can do it, then so can you.

The Illustrations

In the following pages you will find each of the 100 hearts. The invitation is to simply flip through the pages, take some time with each image, and see what comes up for you. Enjoy!

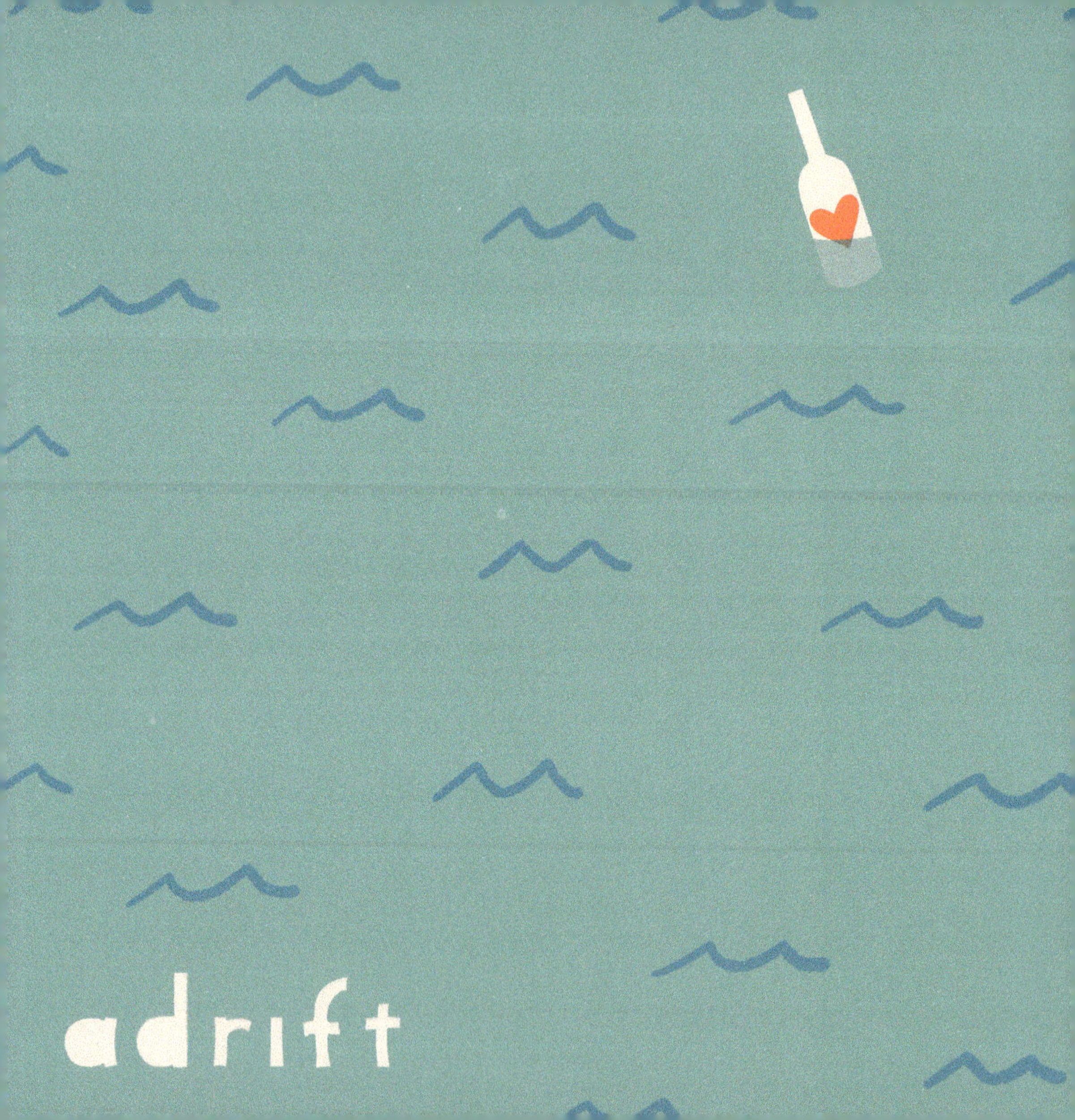
adrift

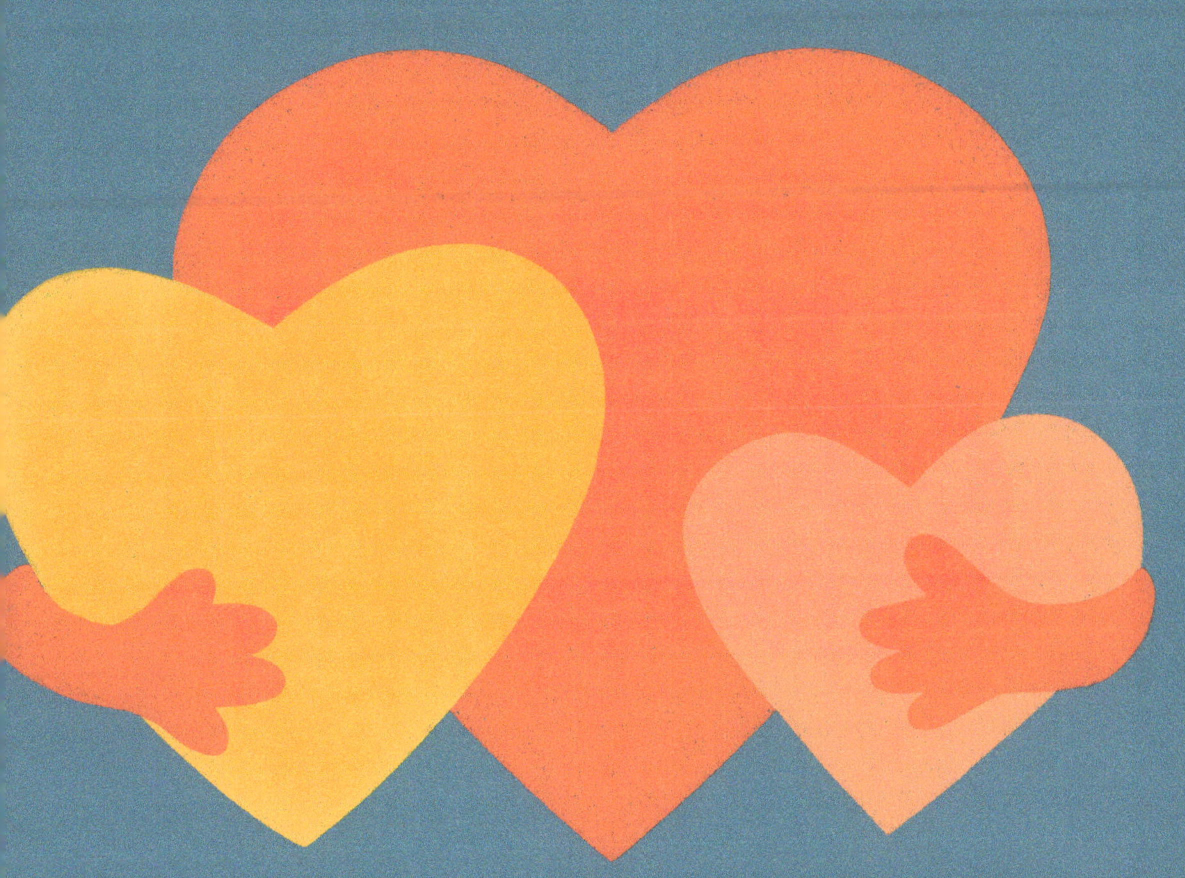

affectionate

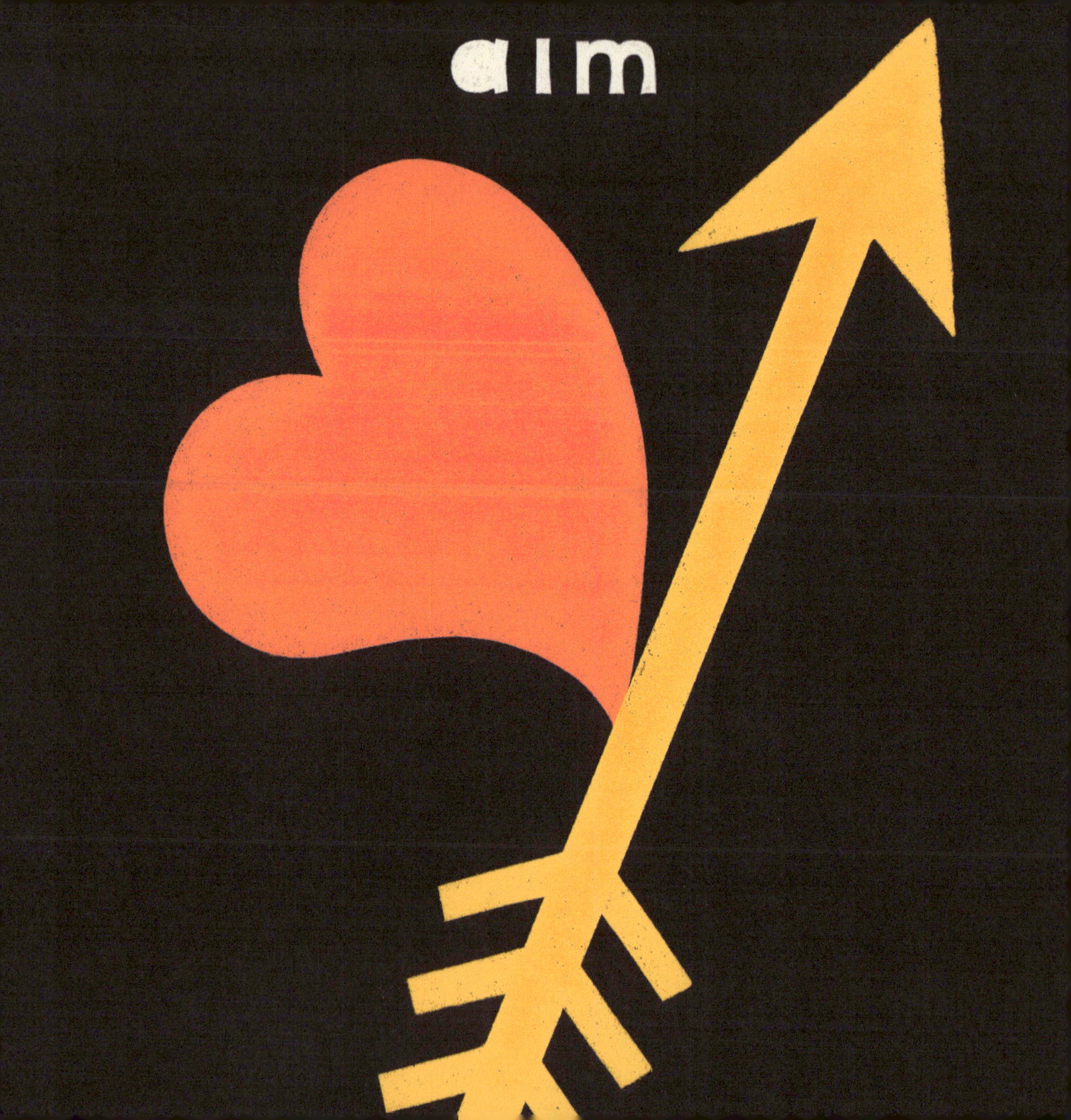
aim

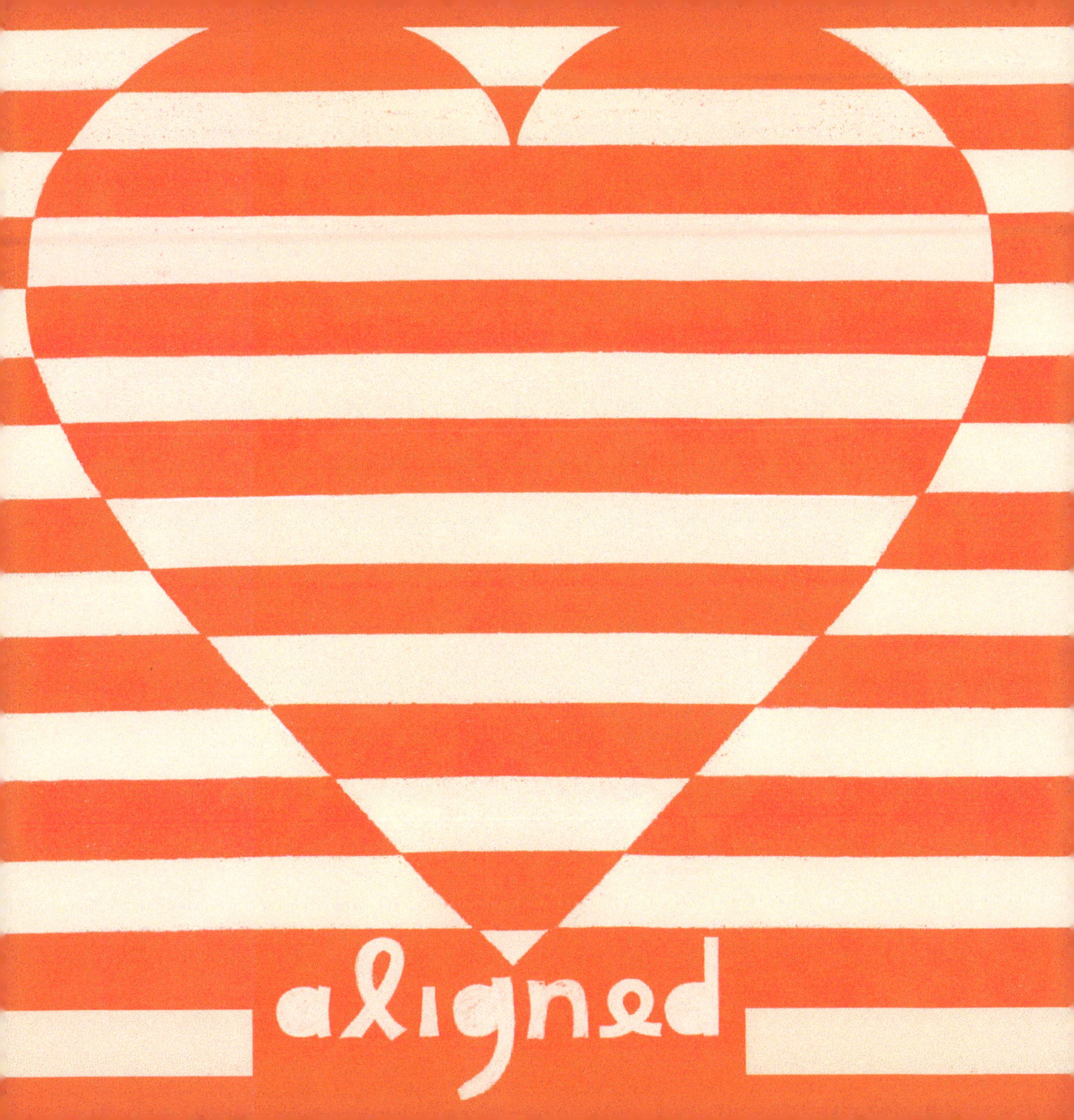
aligned

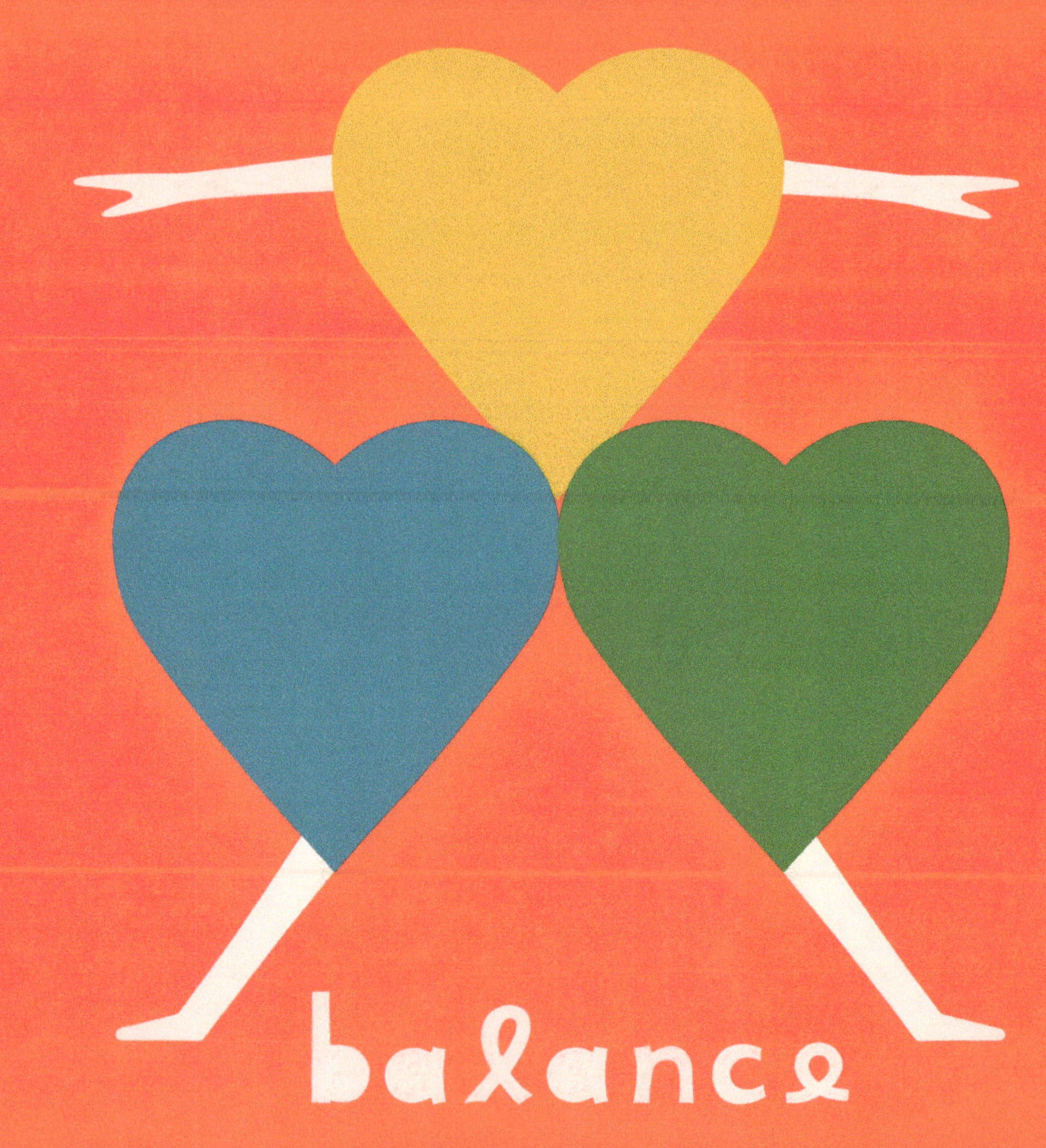

balance

big

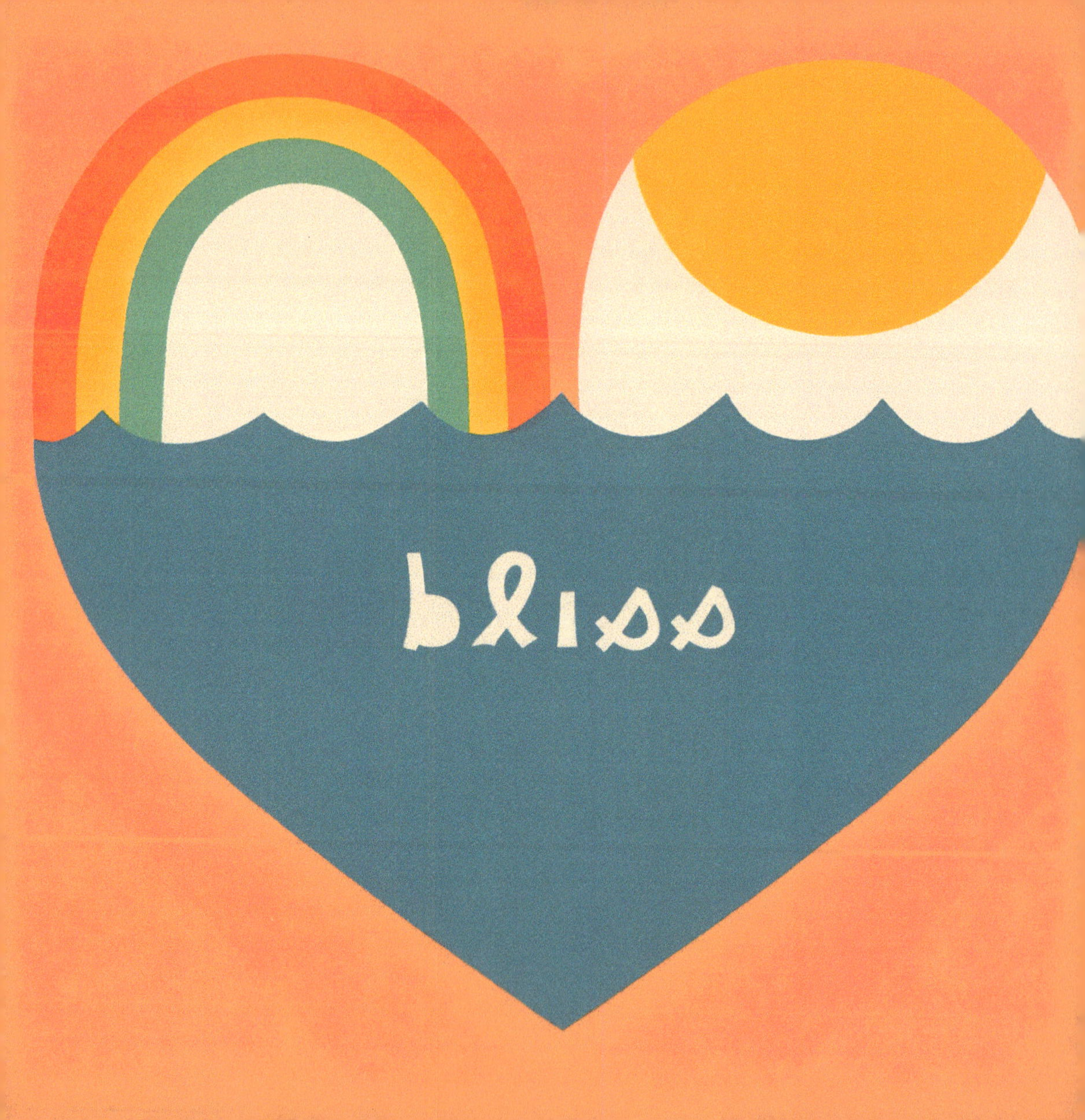

bliss

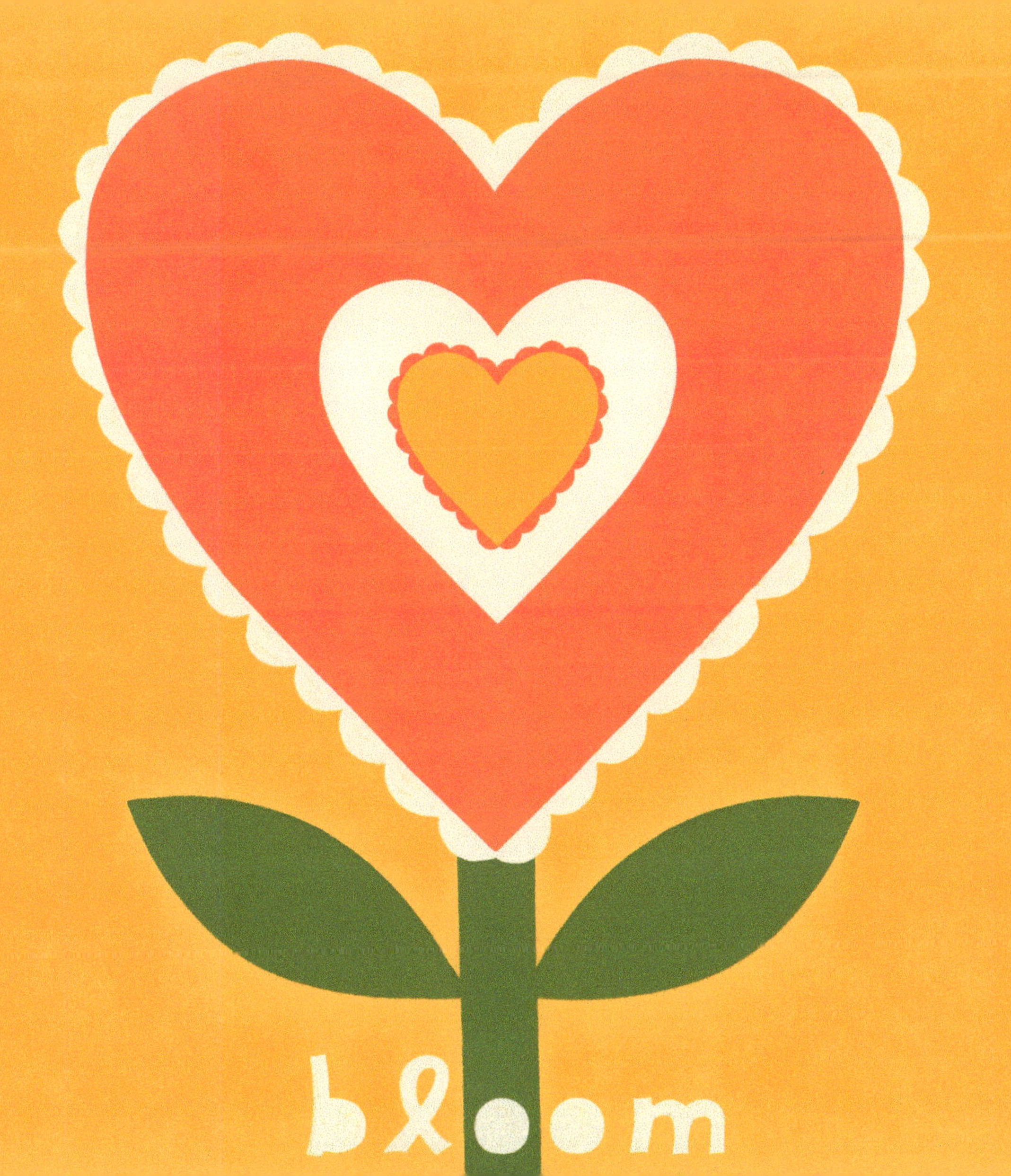

bloom

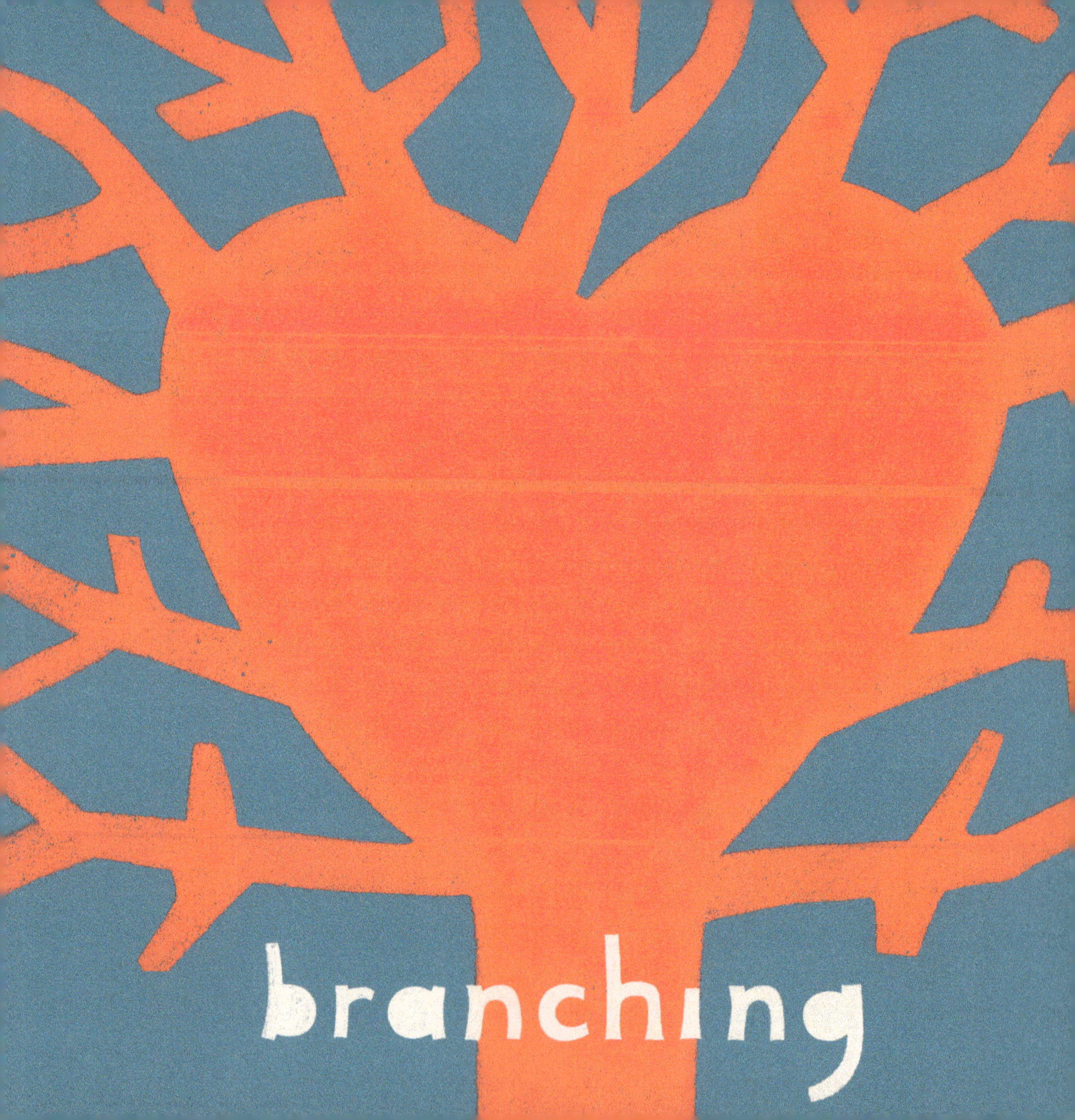
branching

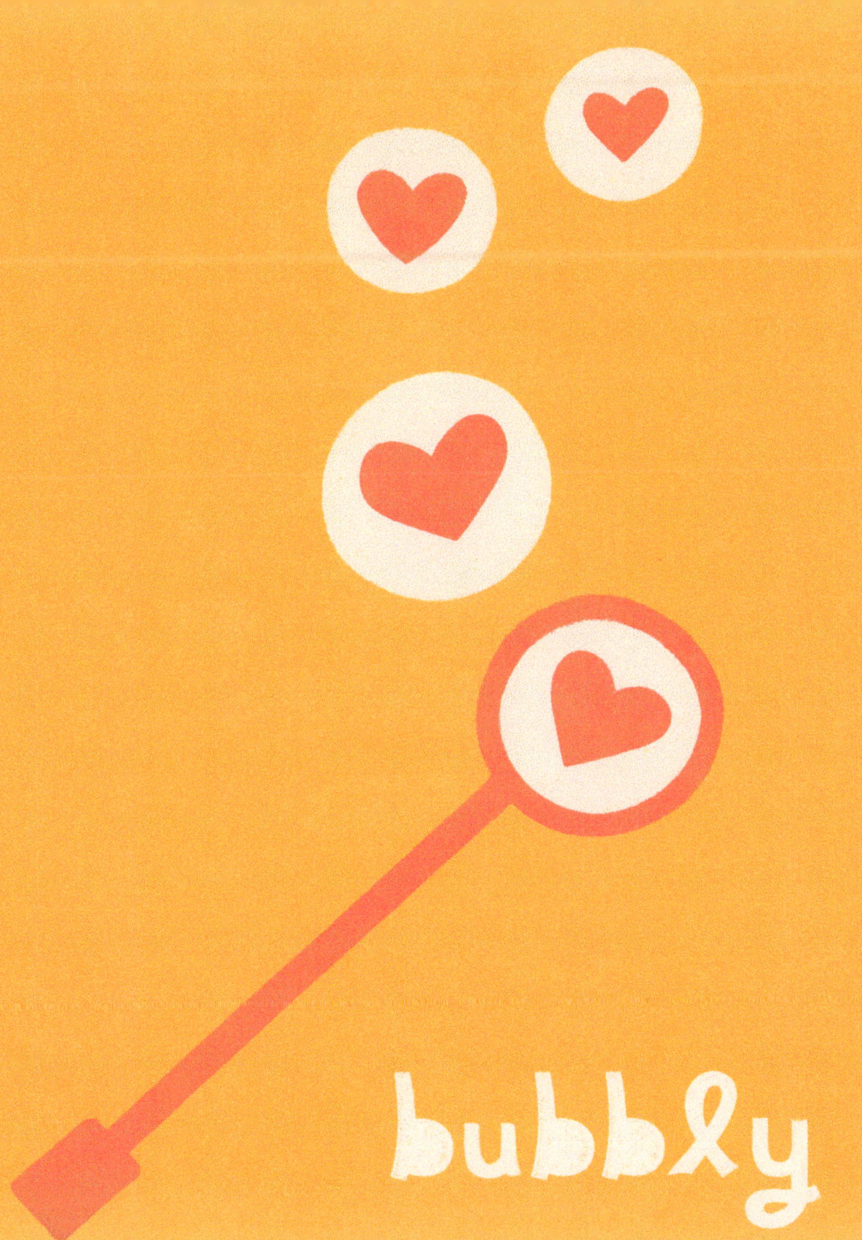
bubbly

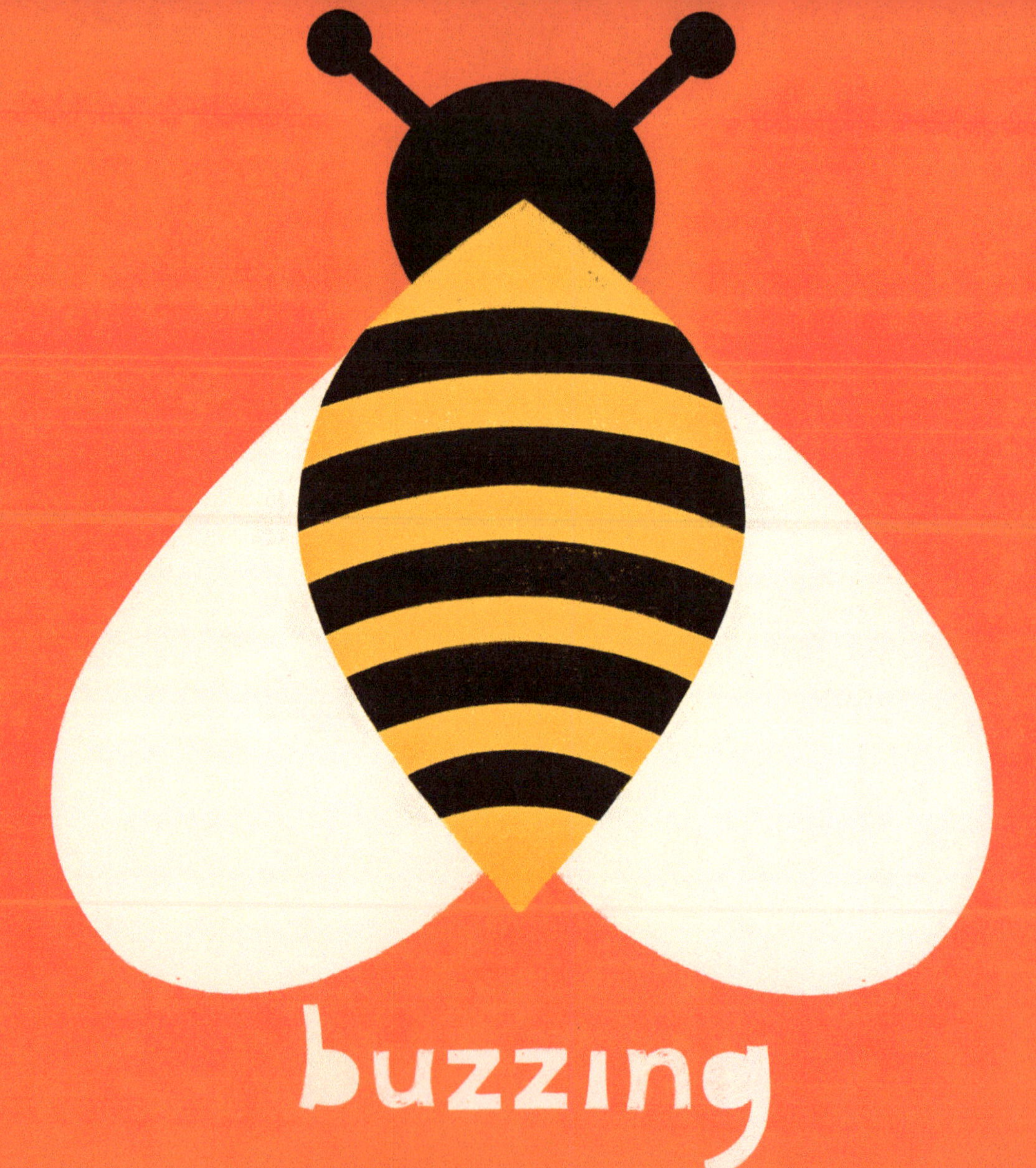
buzzing

calm

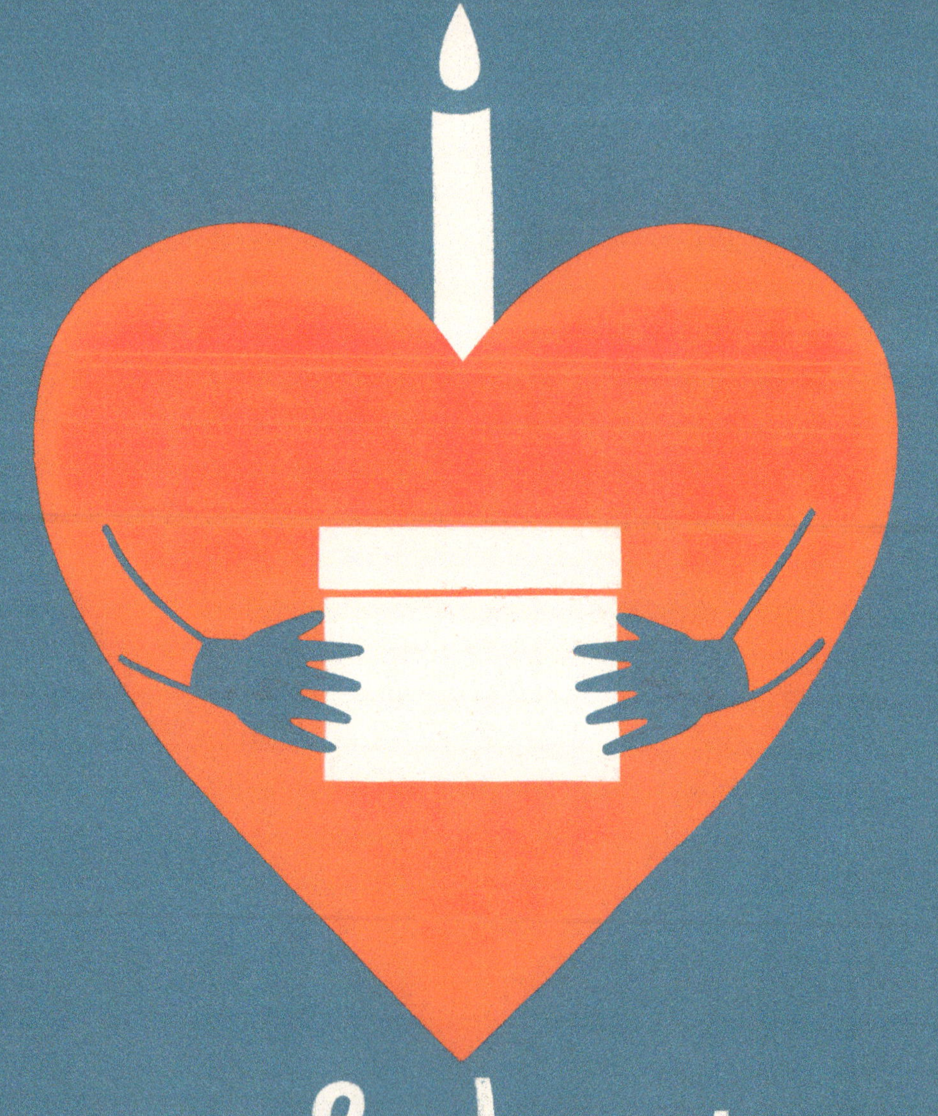
celebrate

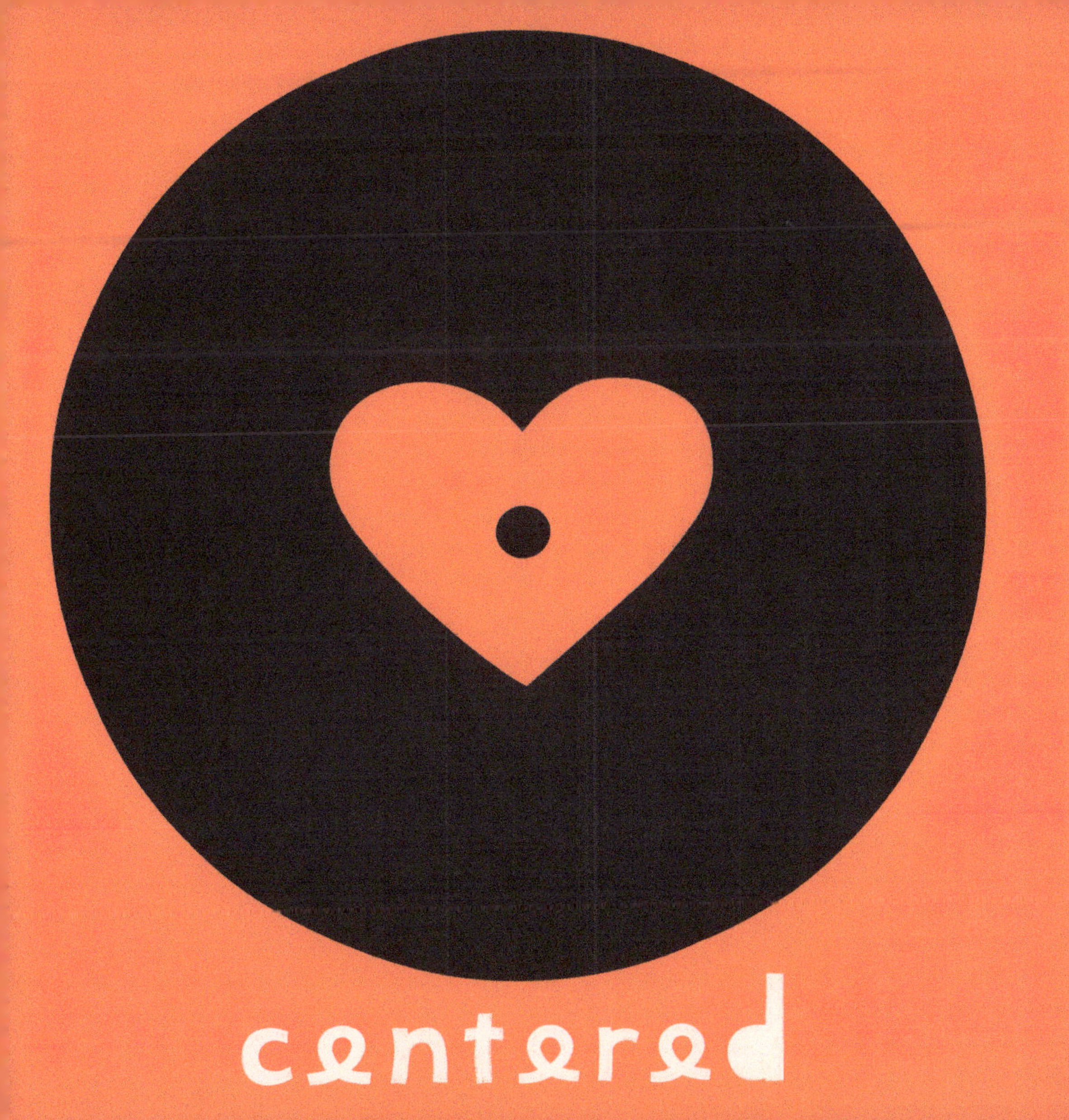
centered

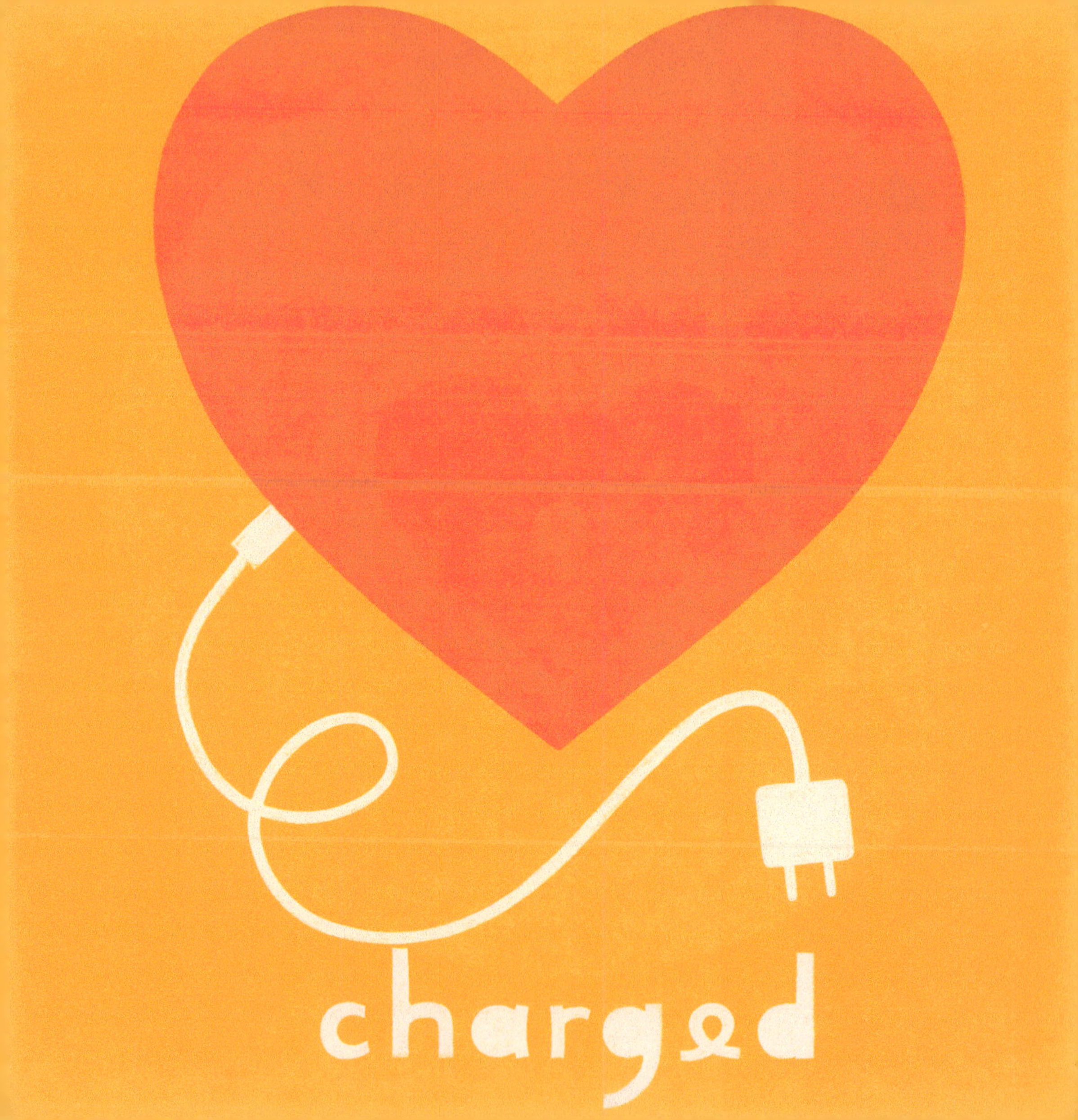
charged

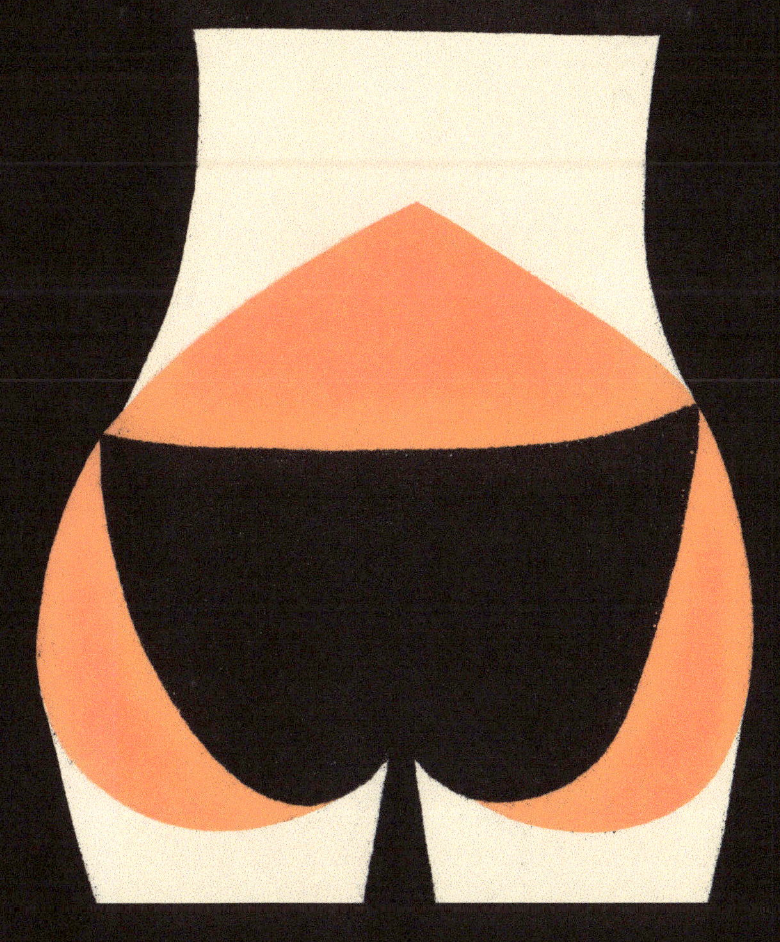

cheeky

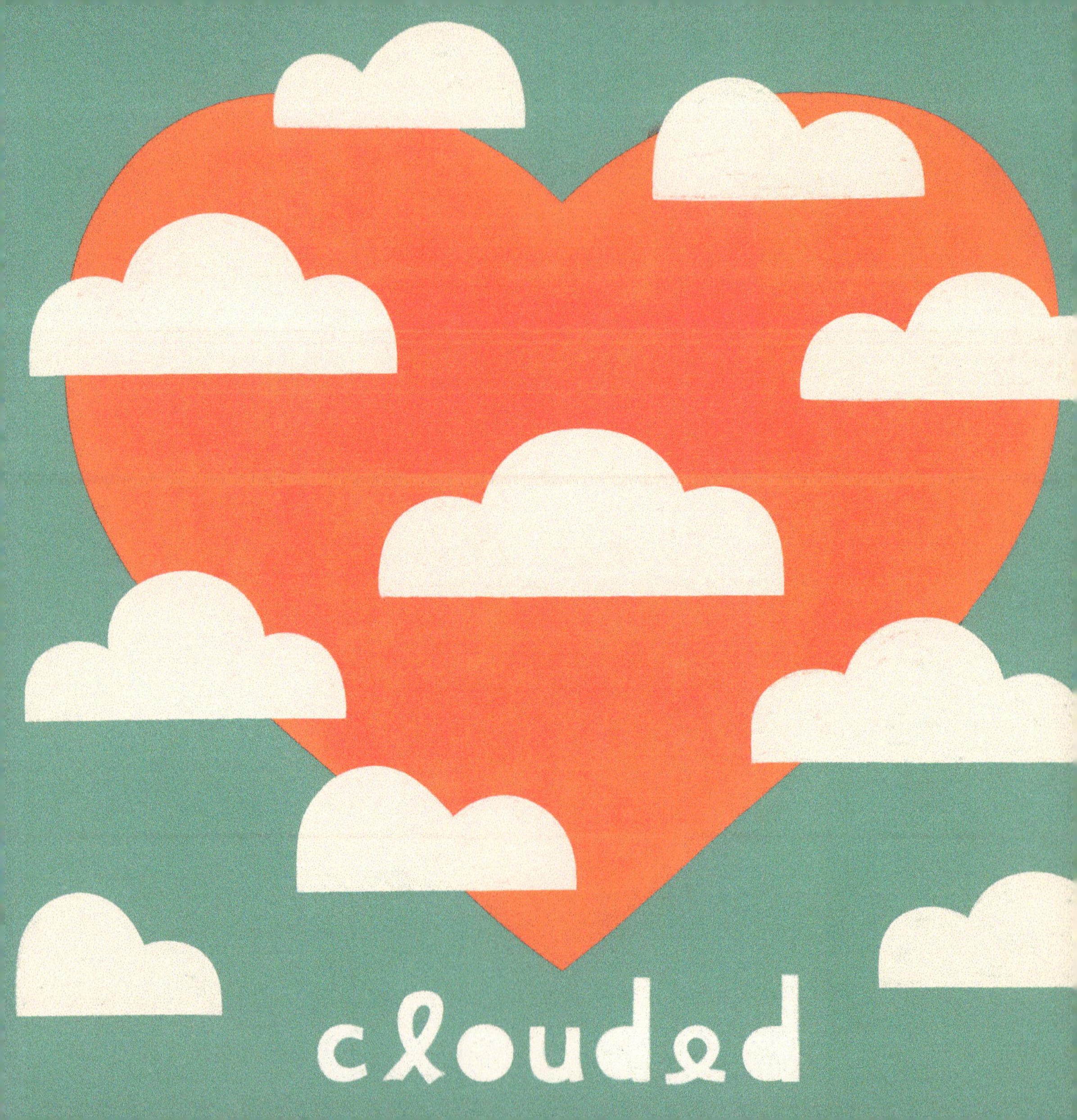

clouded

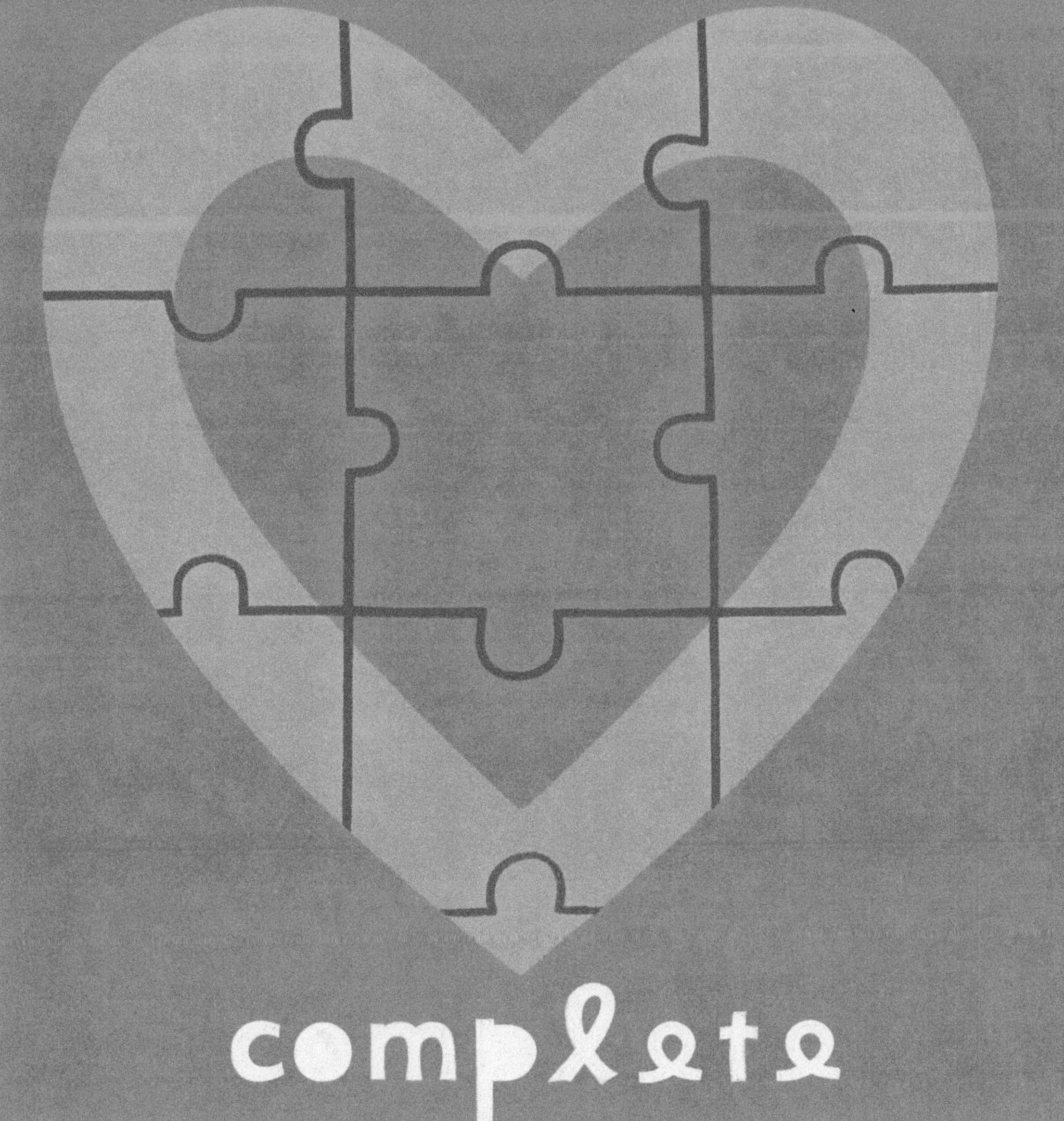
complete

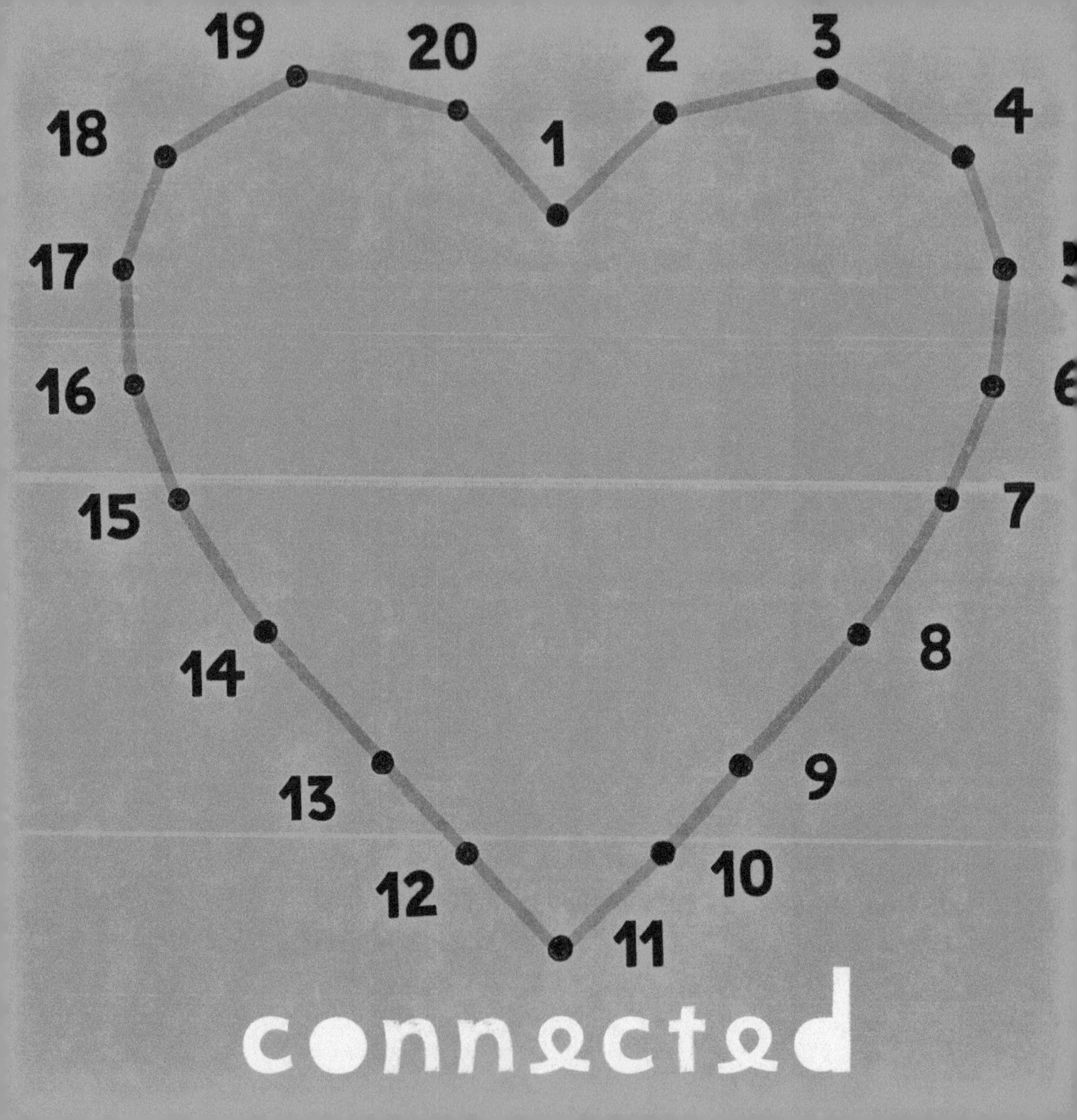

19
20
2
3
18
1
4
17
5
16
6
15
7
14
8
13
9
12
10
11
connected

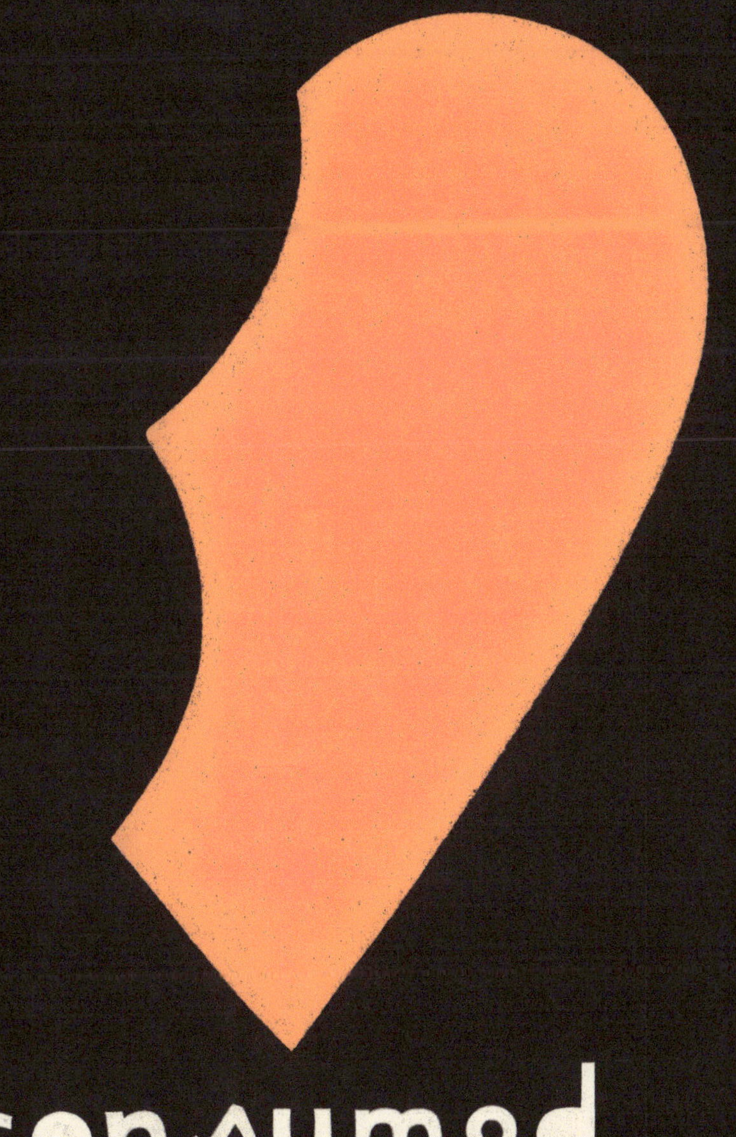
consumed

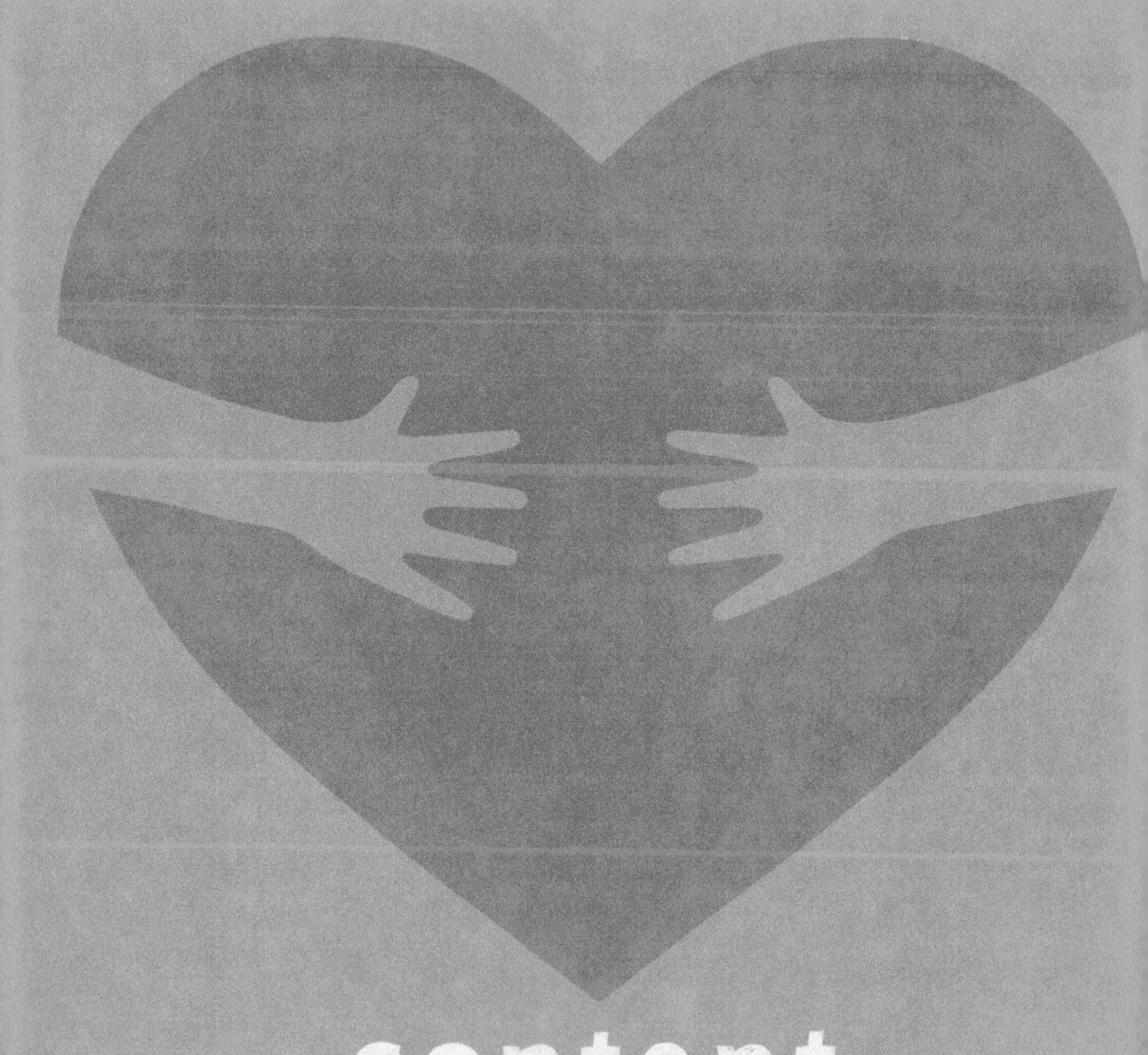
content

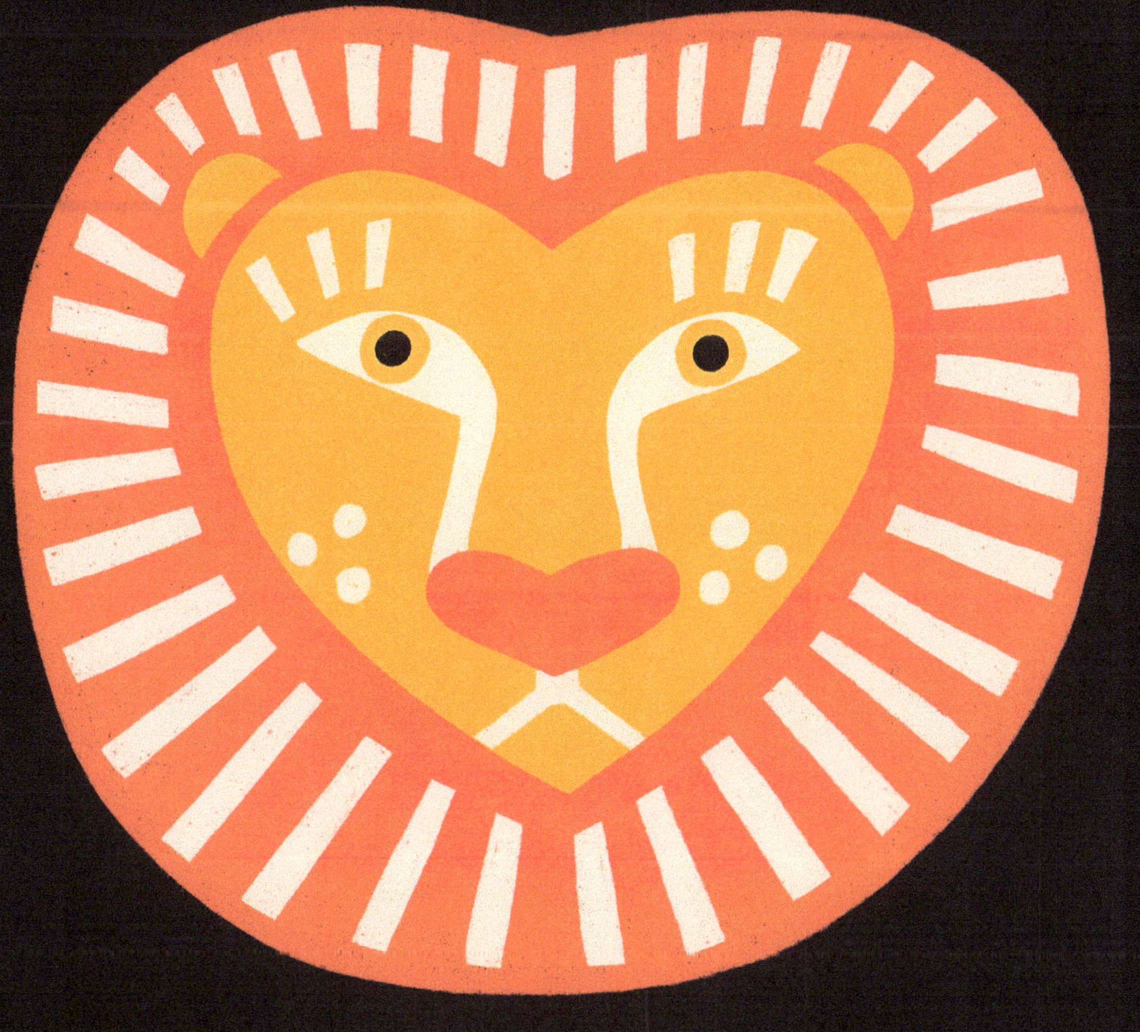
courage

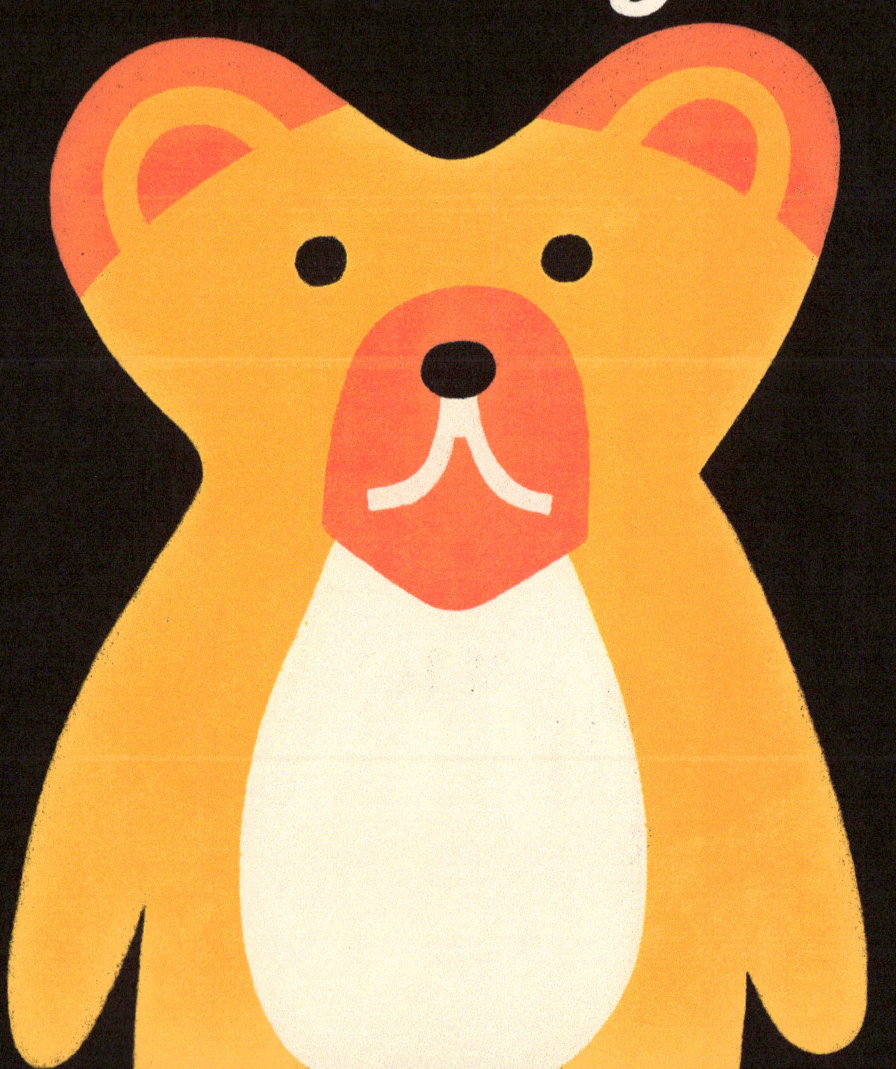

cuddly

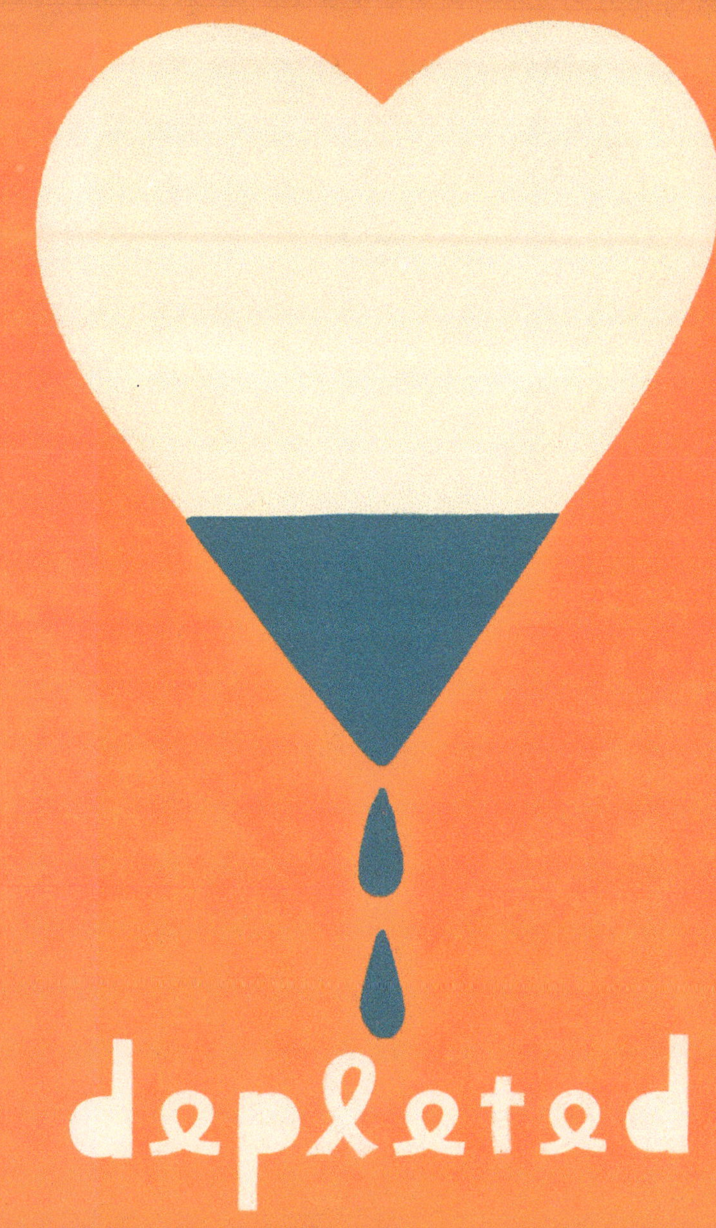

depleted

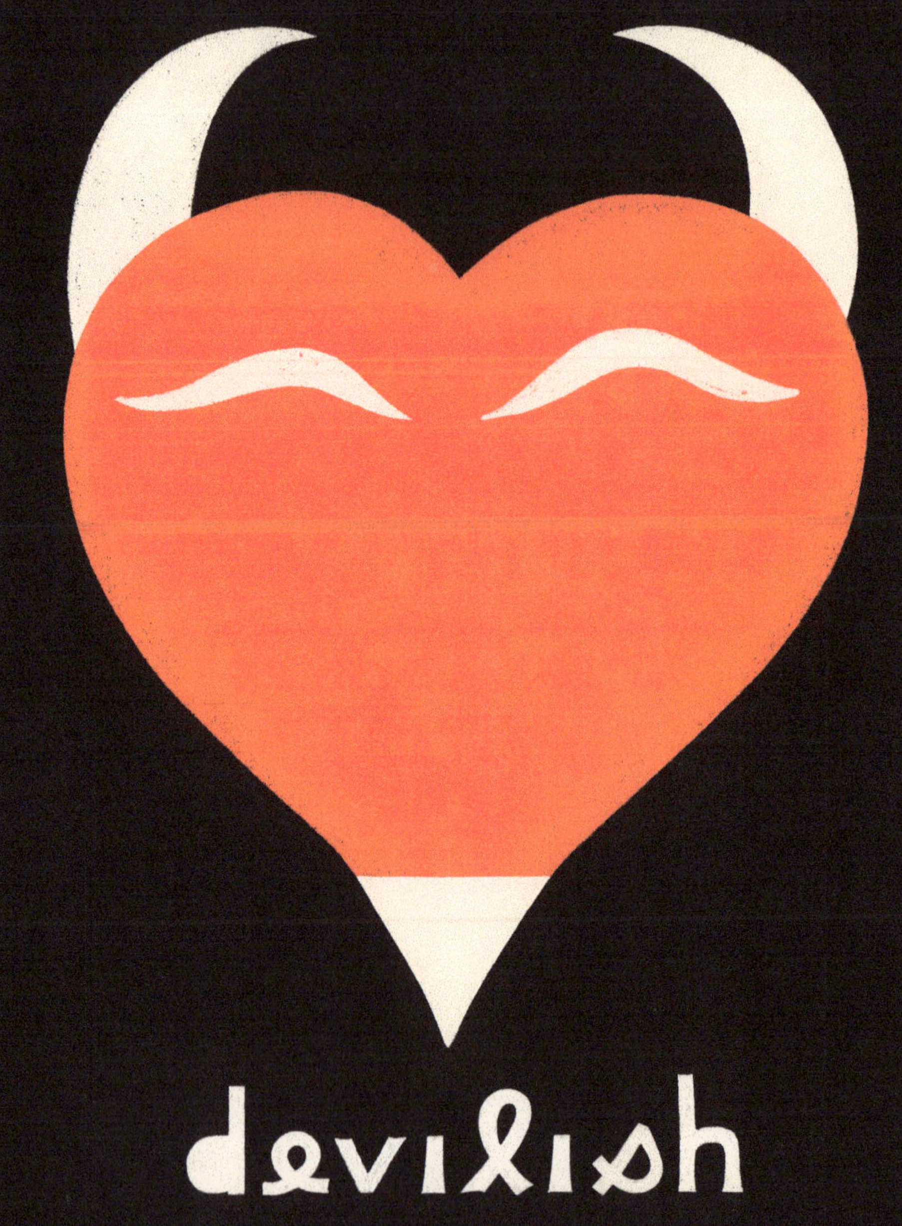

devilish

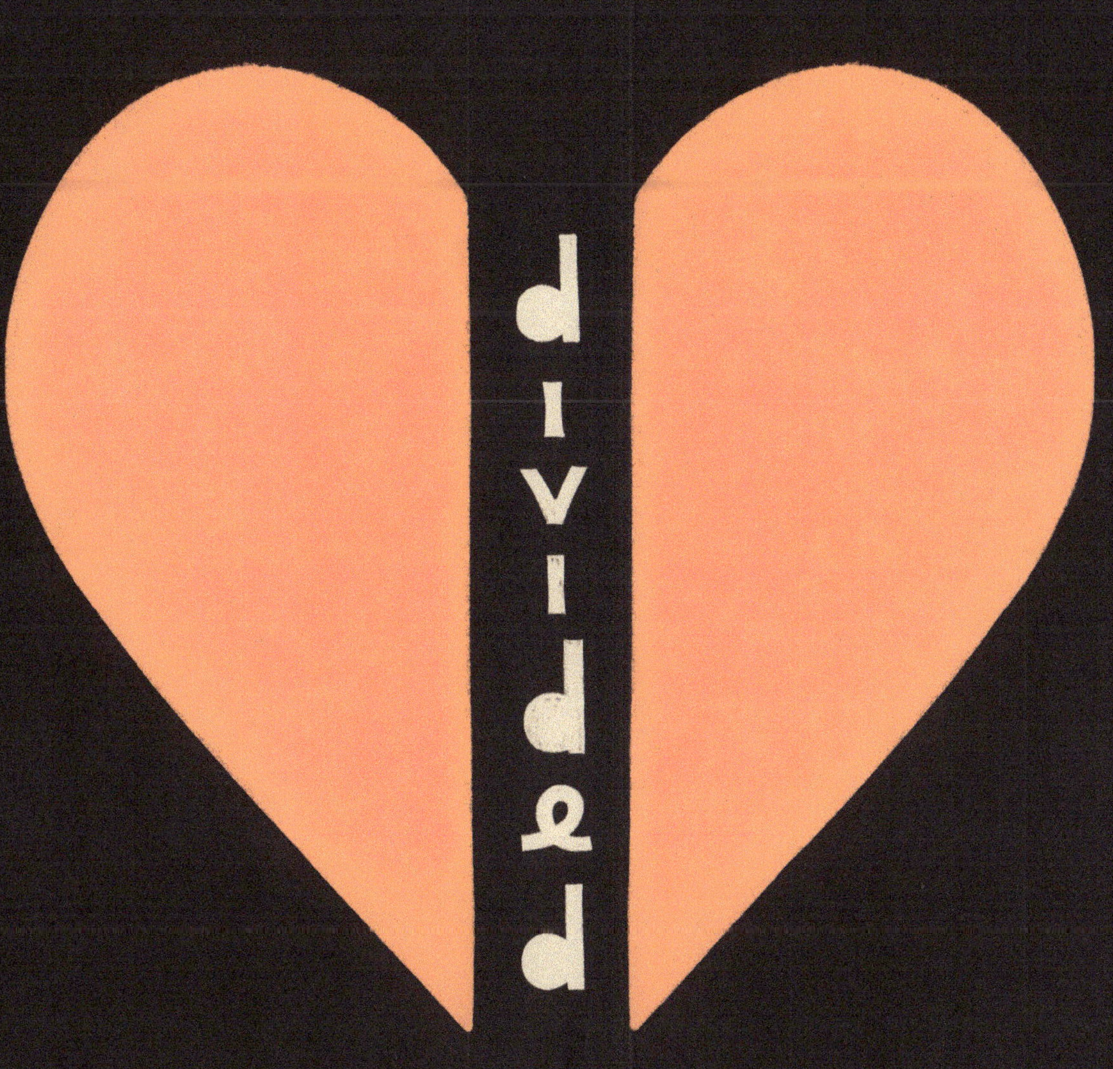

divided

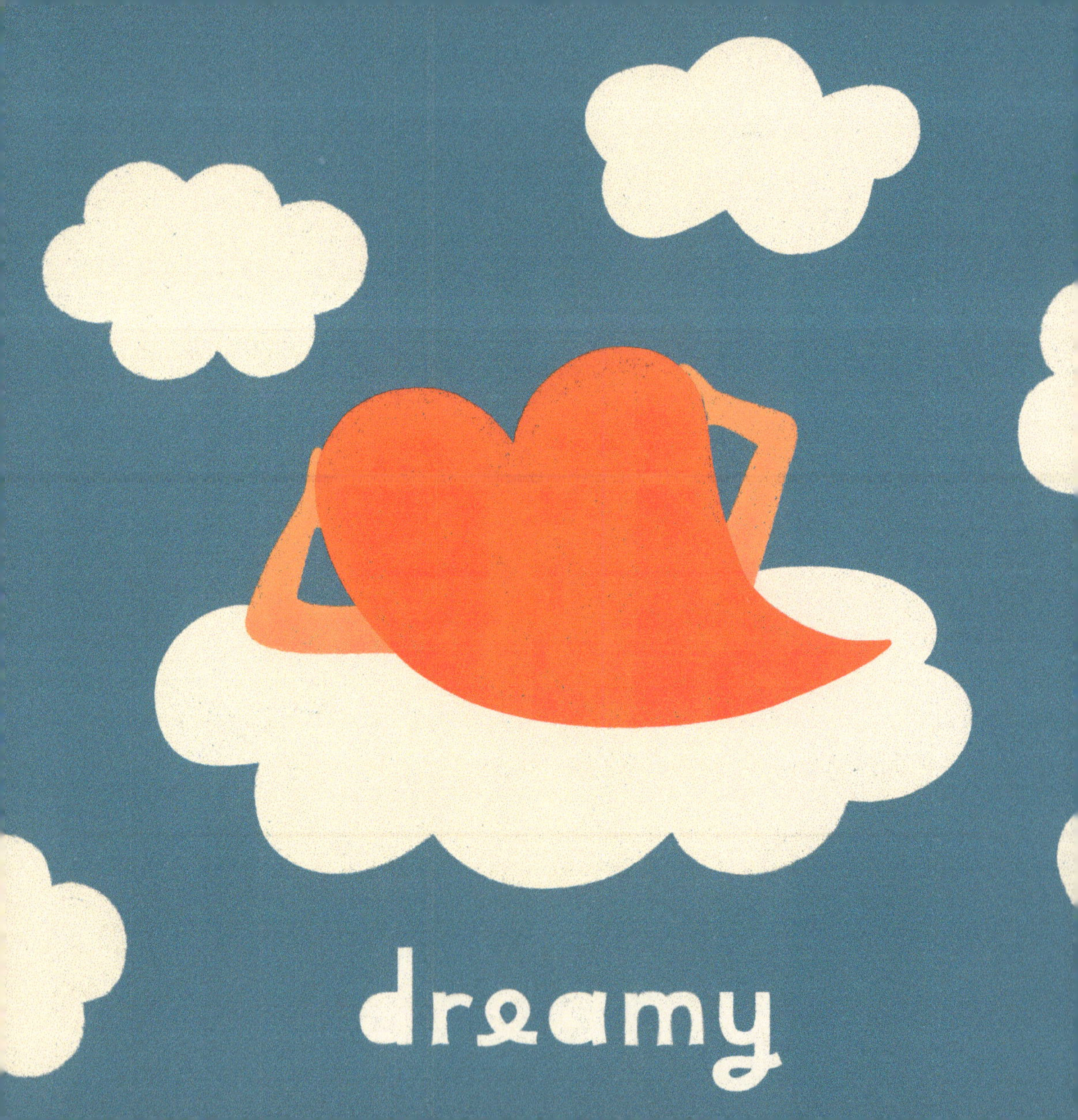
dreamy

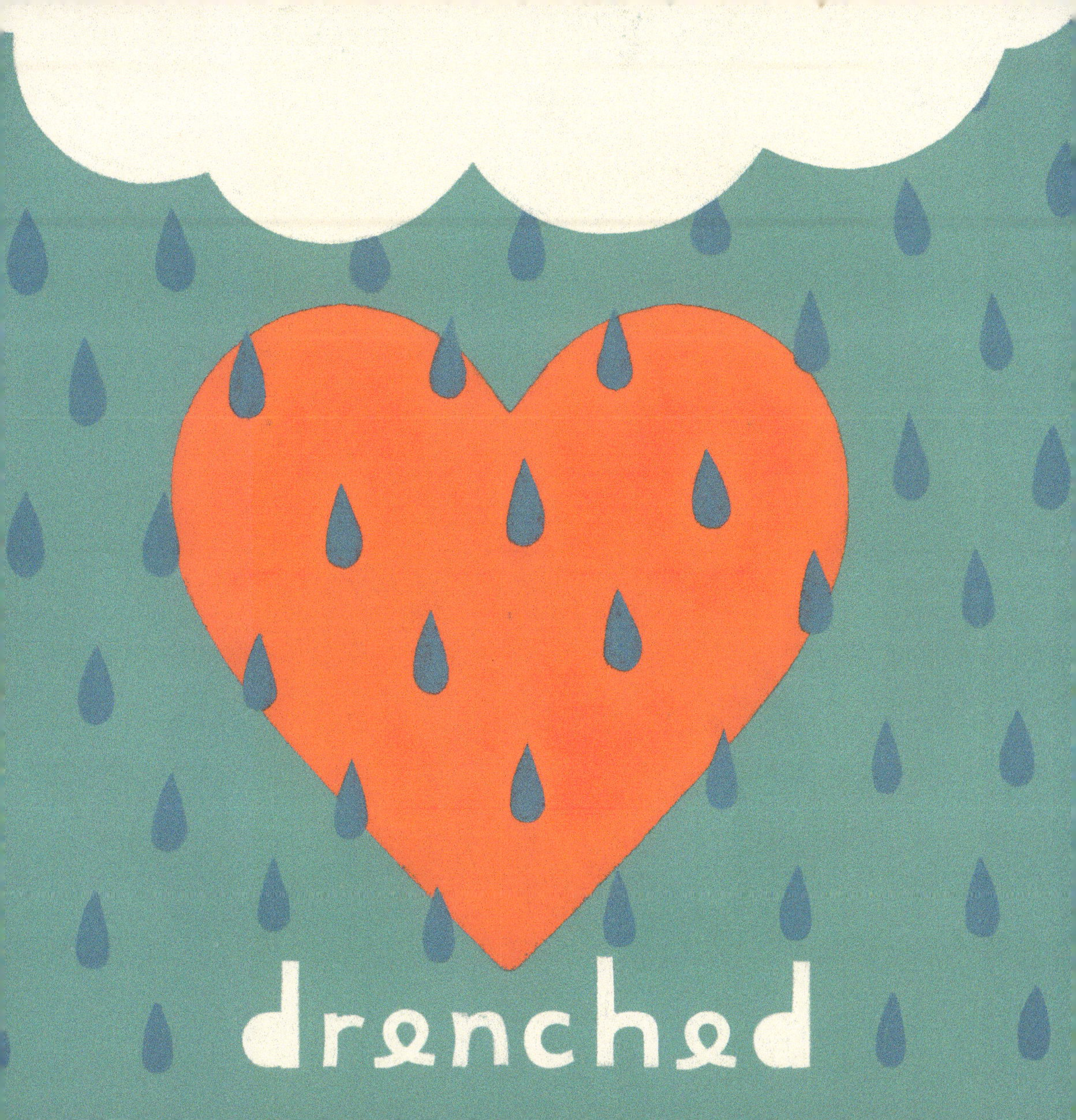

drenched

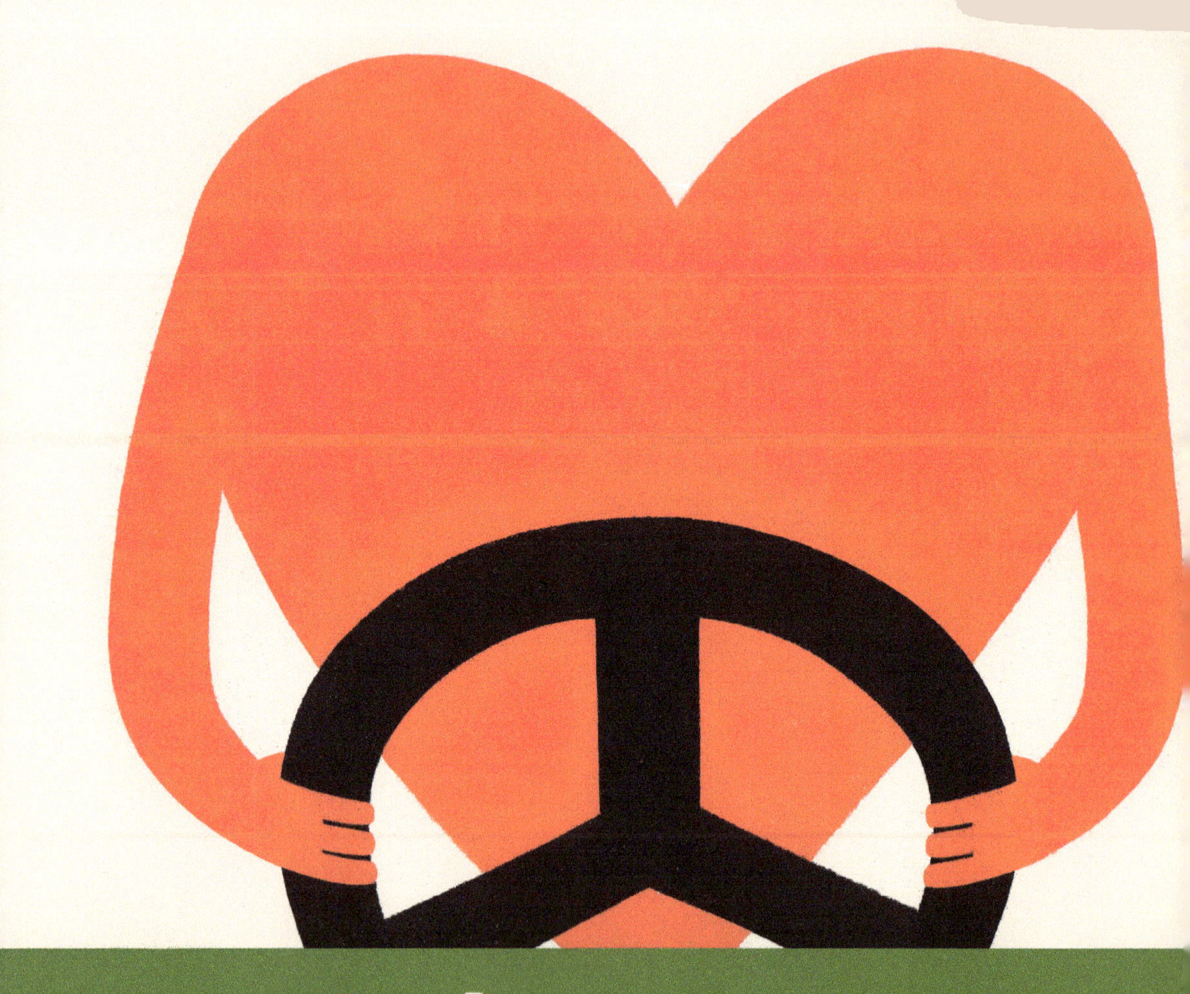

driven

embrace

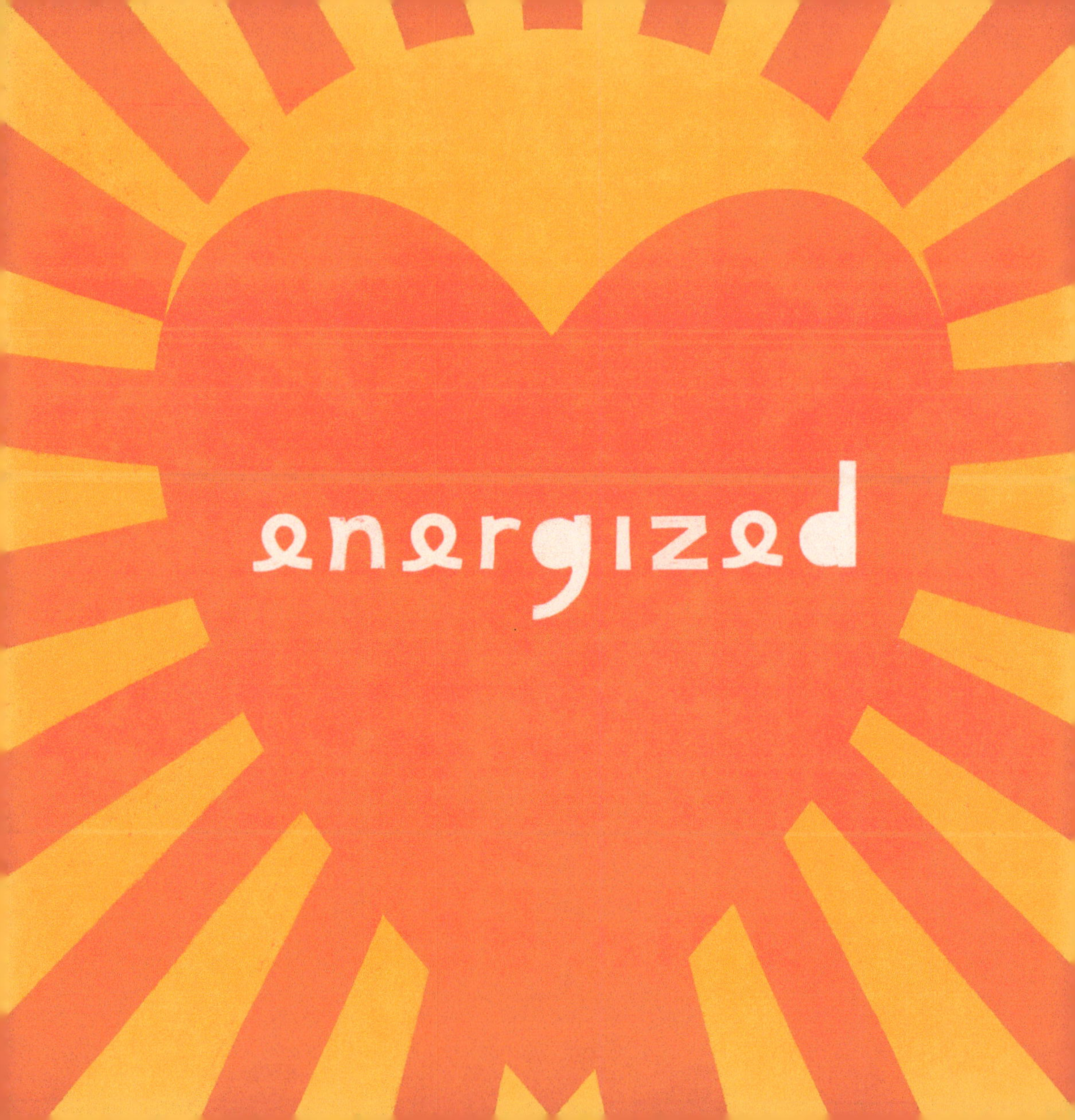

energized

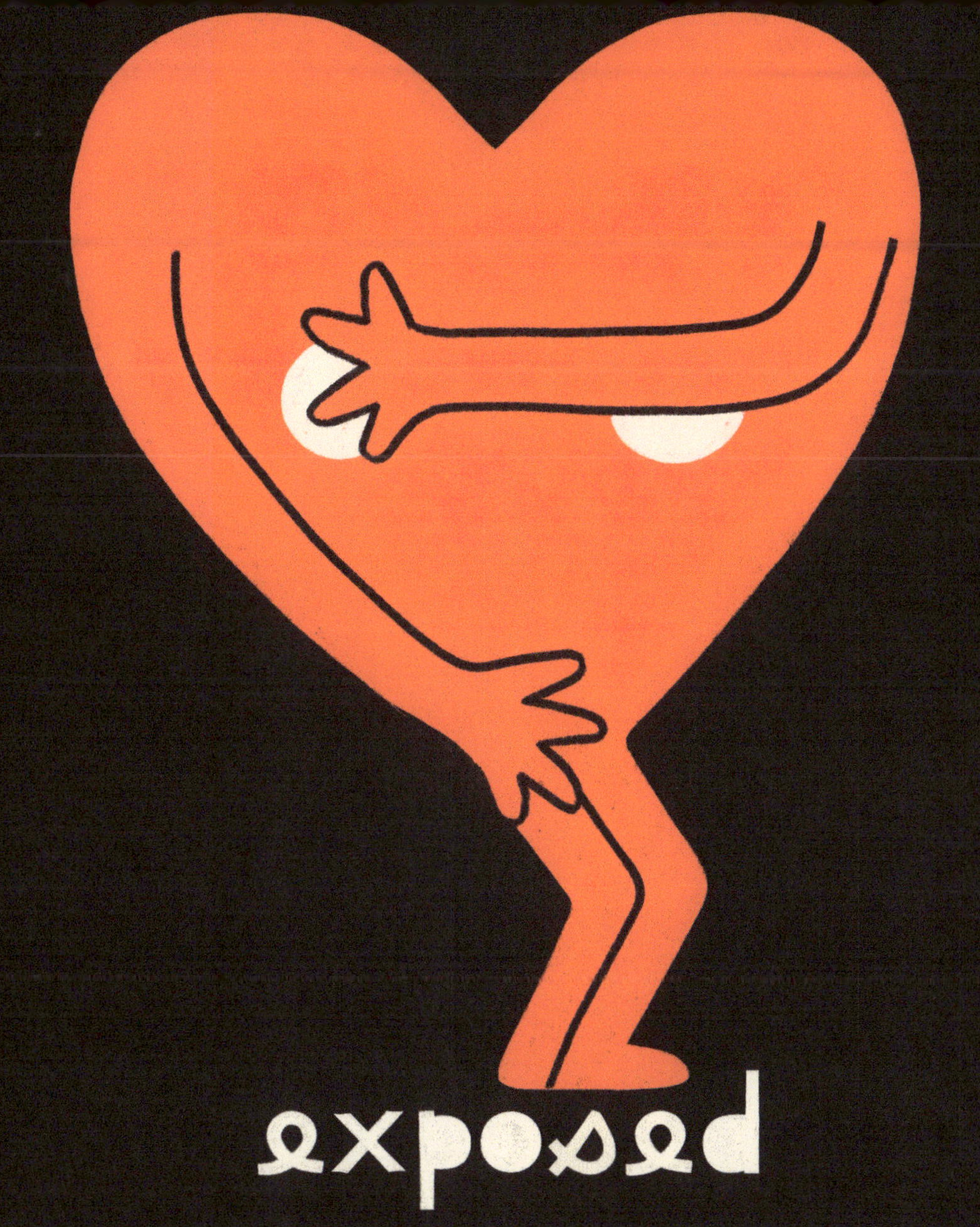
exposed

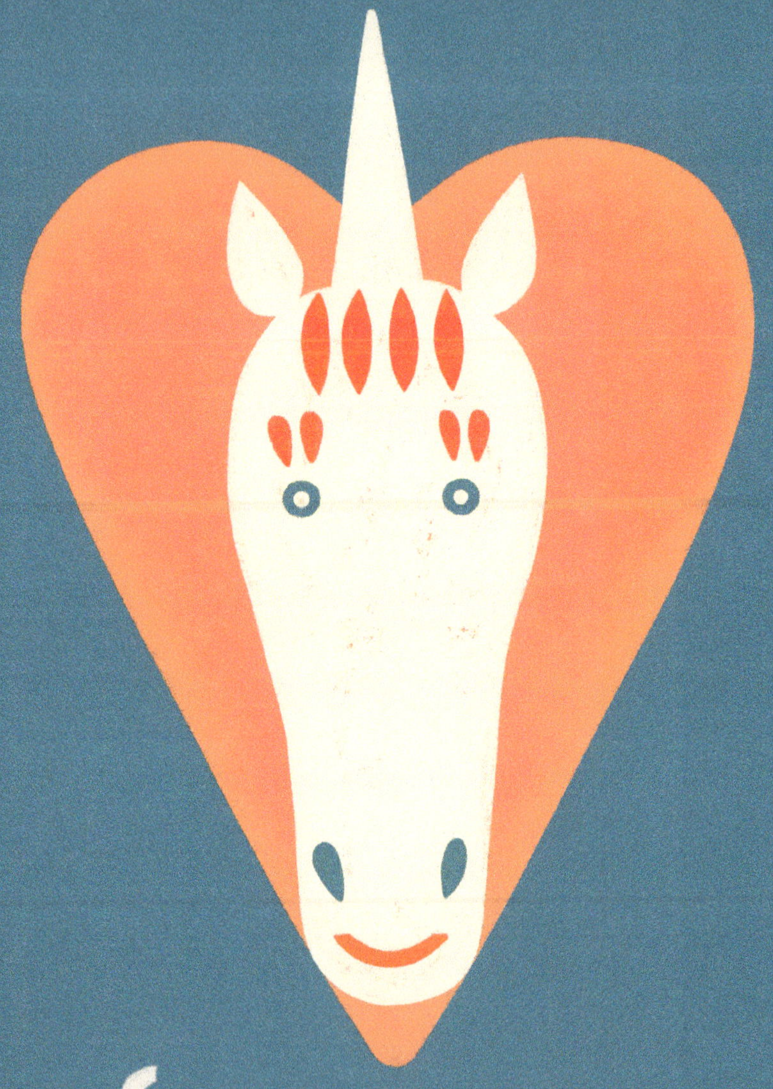

fantastic

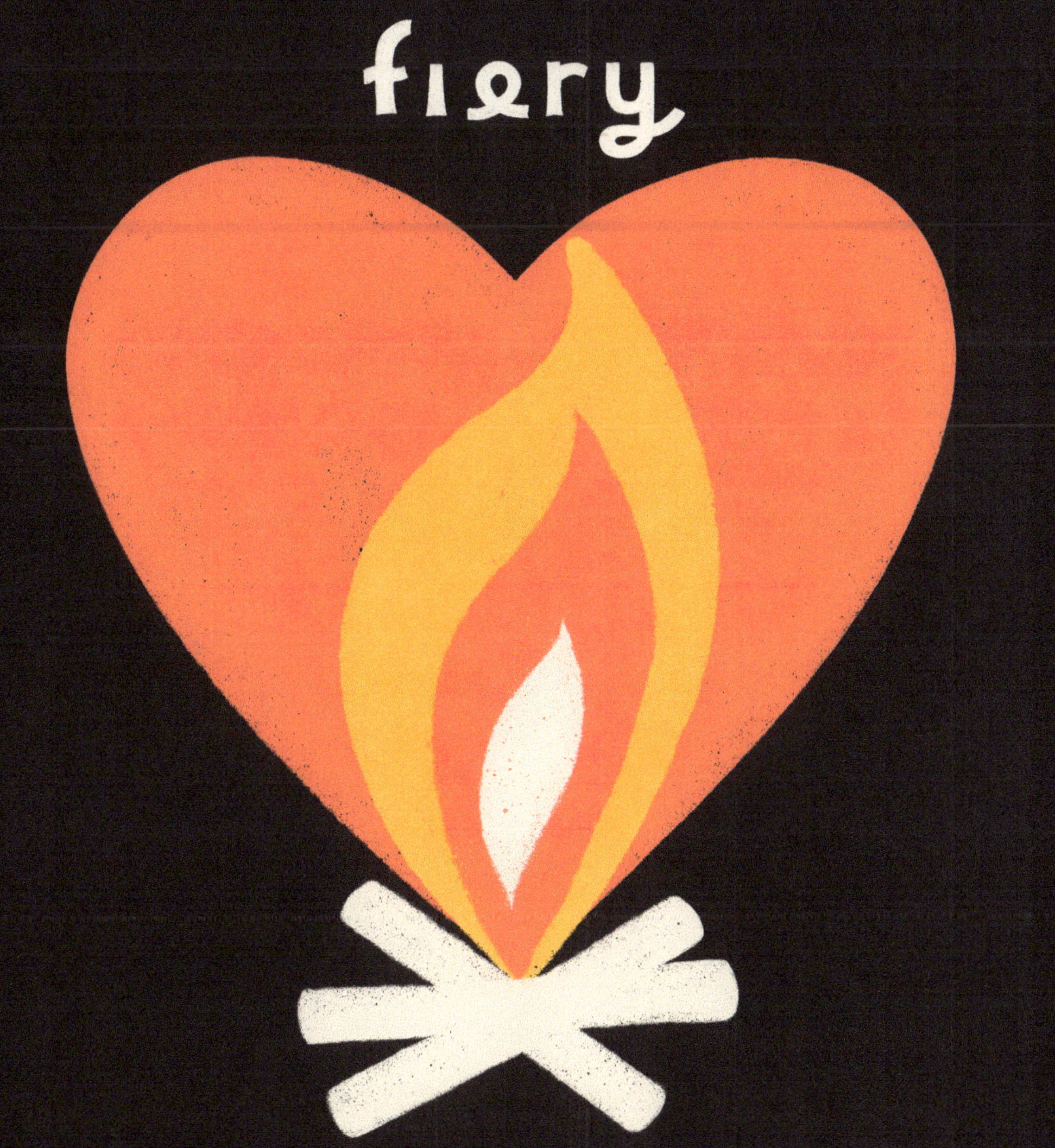

fiery

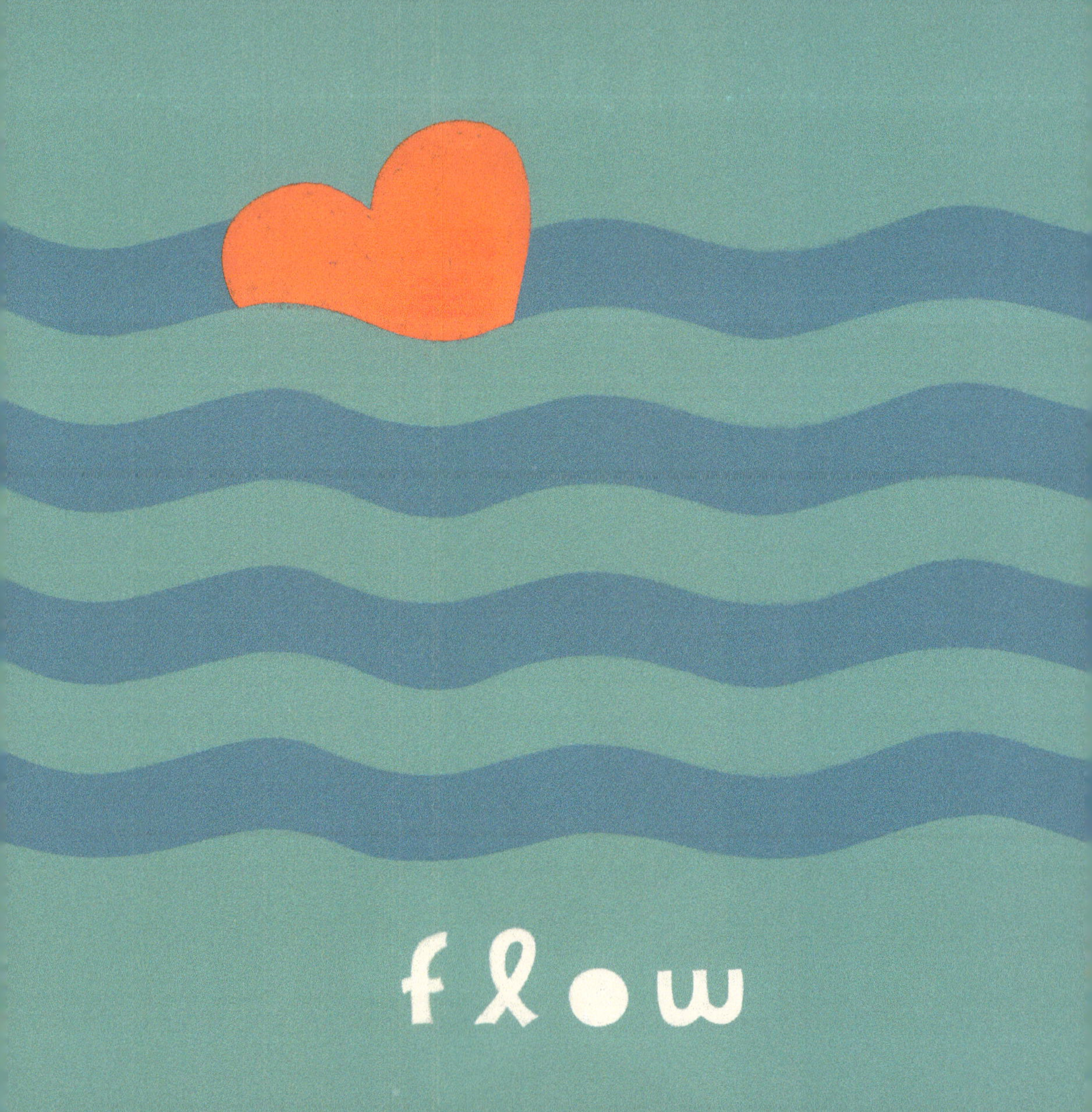
flow

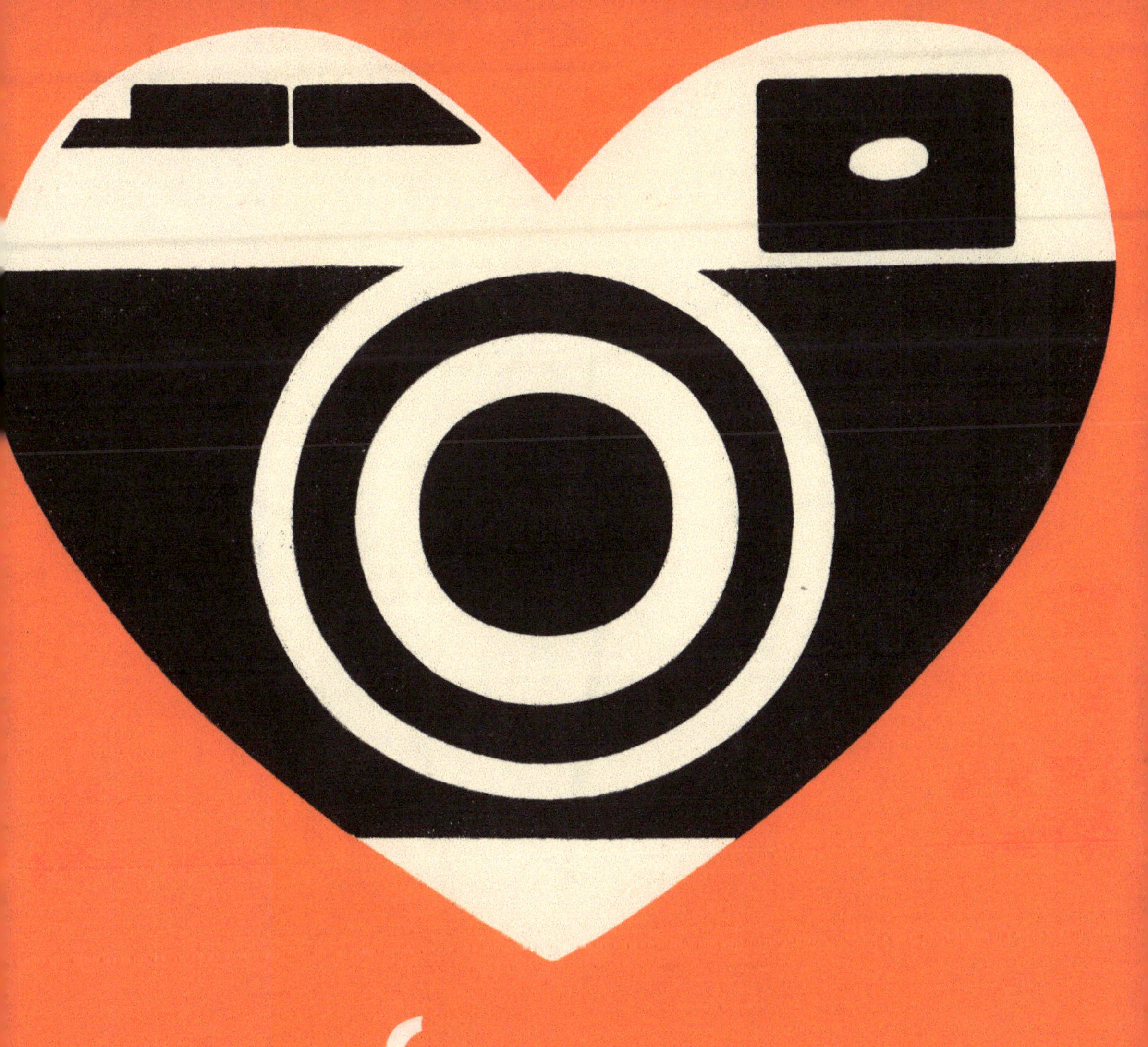
focus

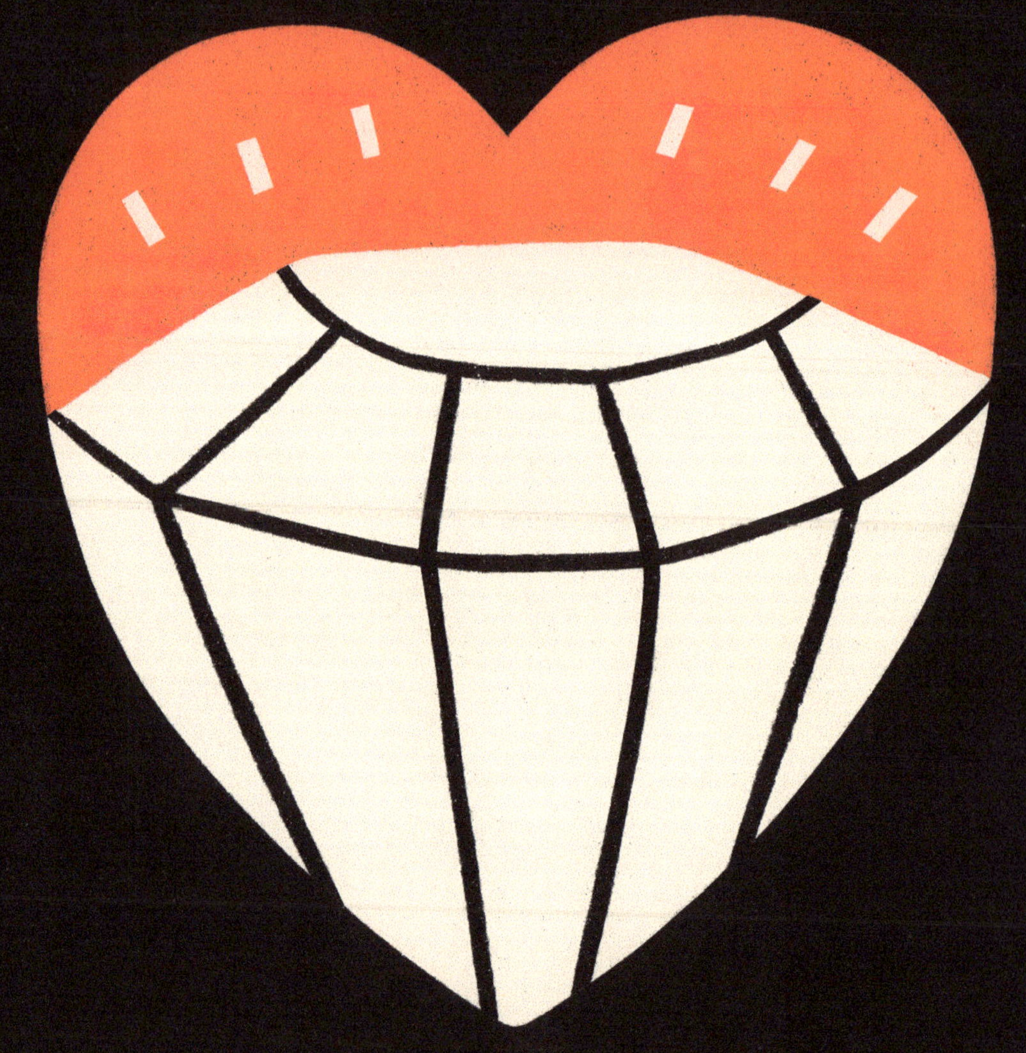
forever

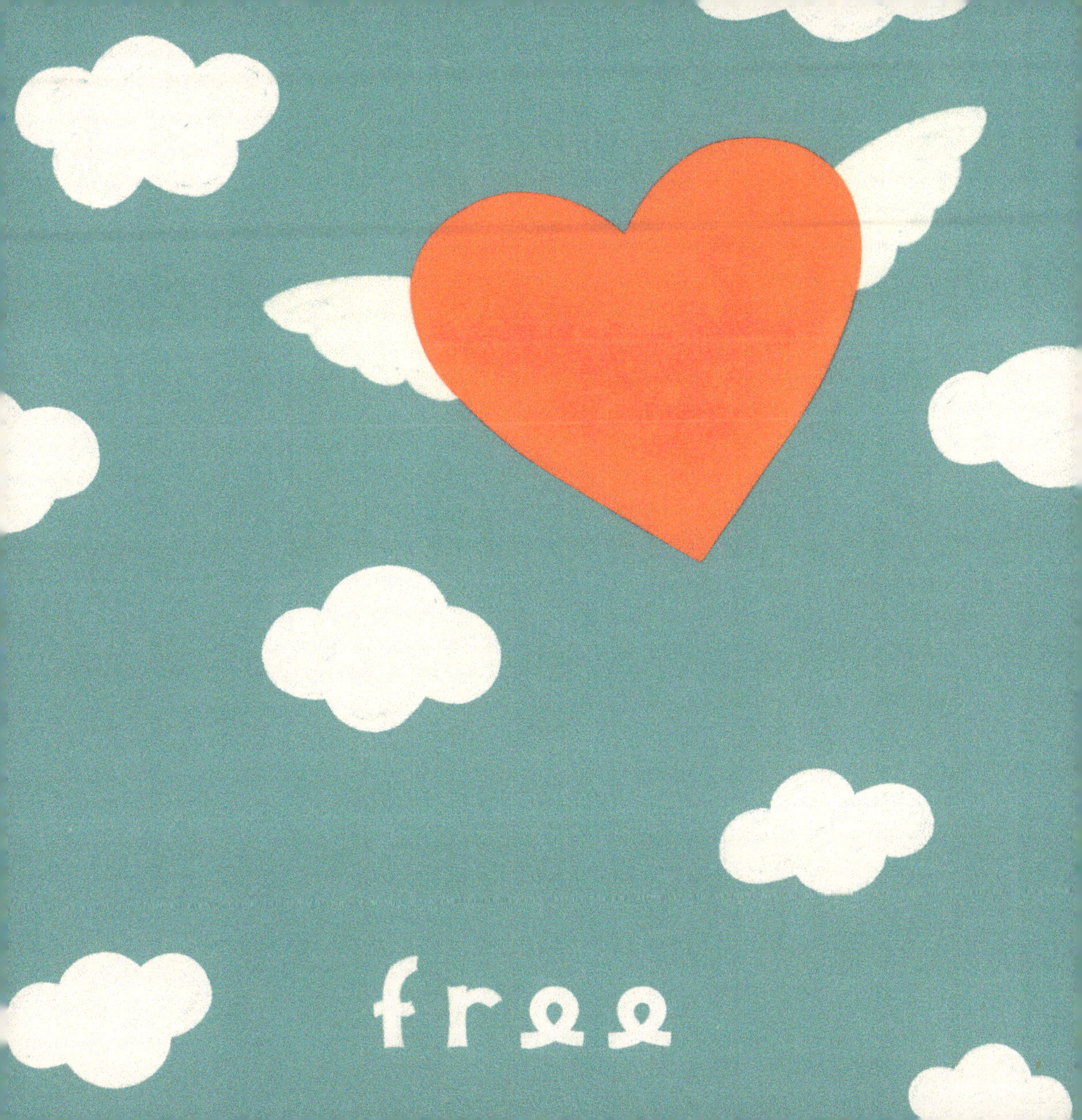

free

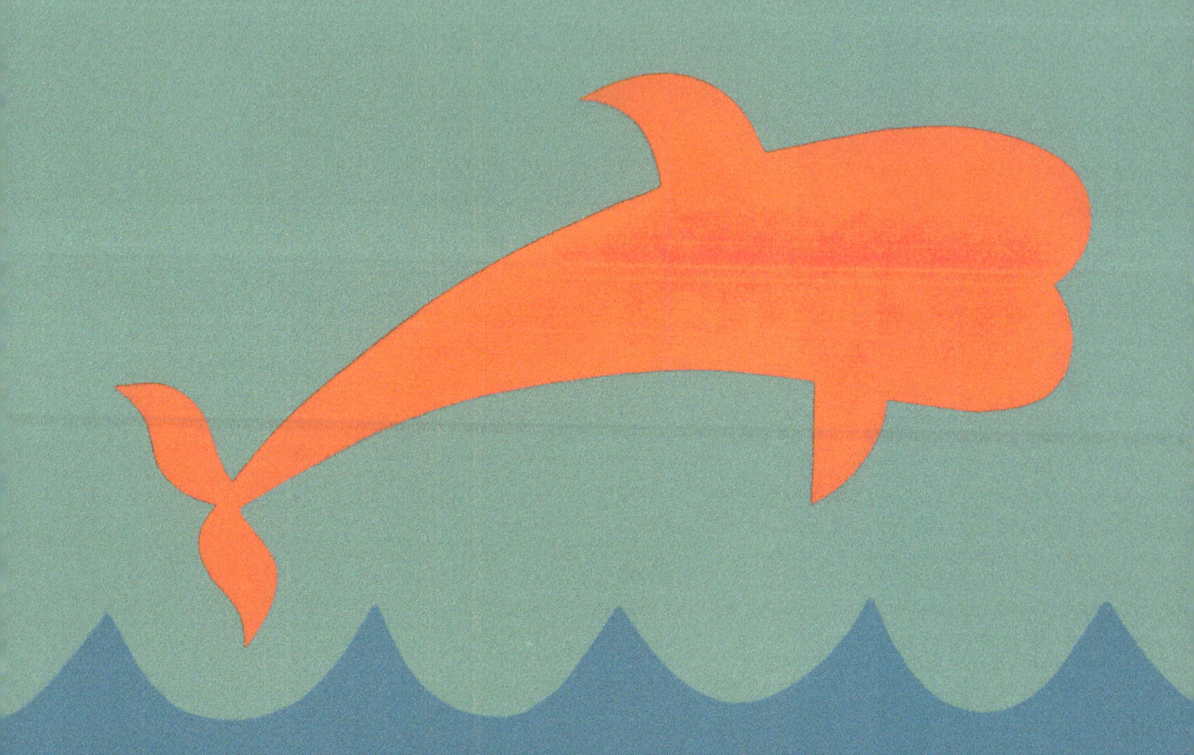

frolick

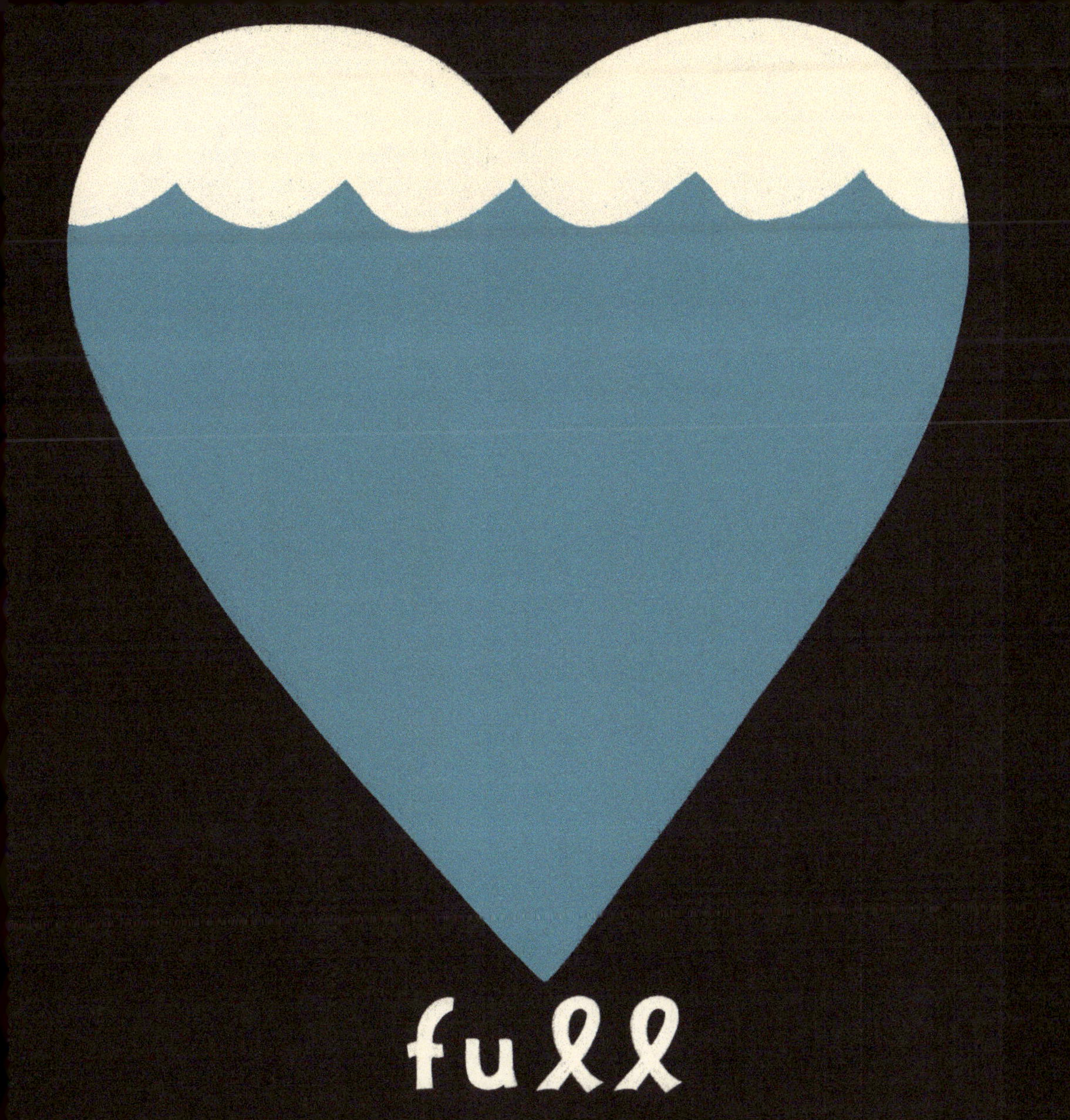
full

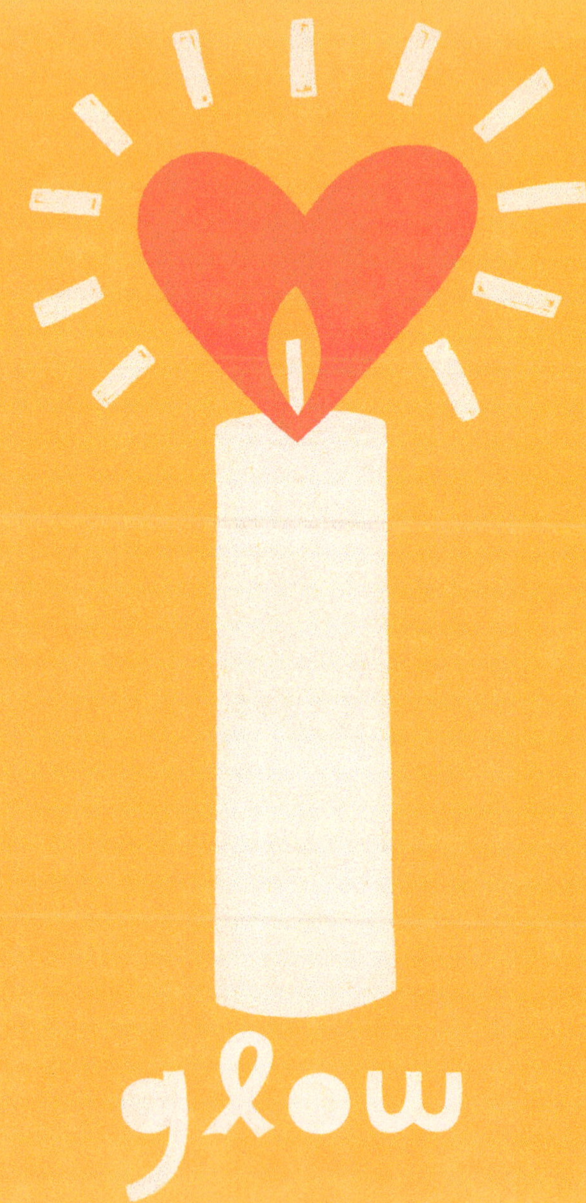

glow

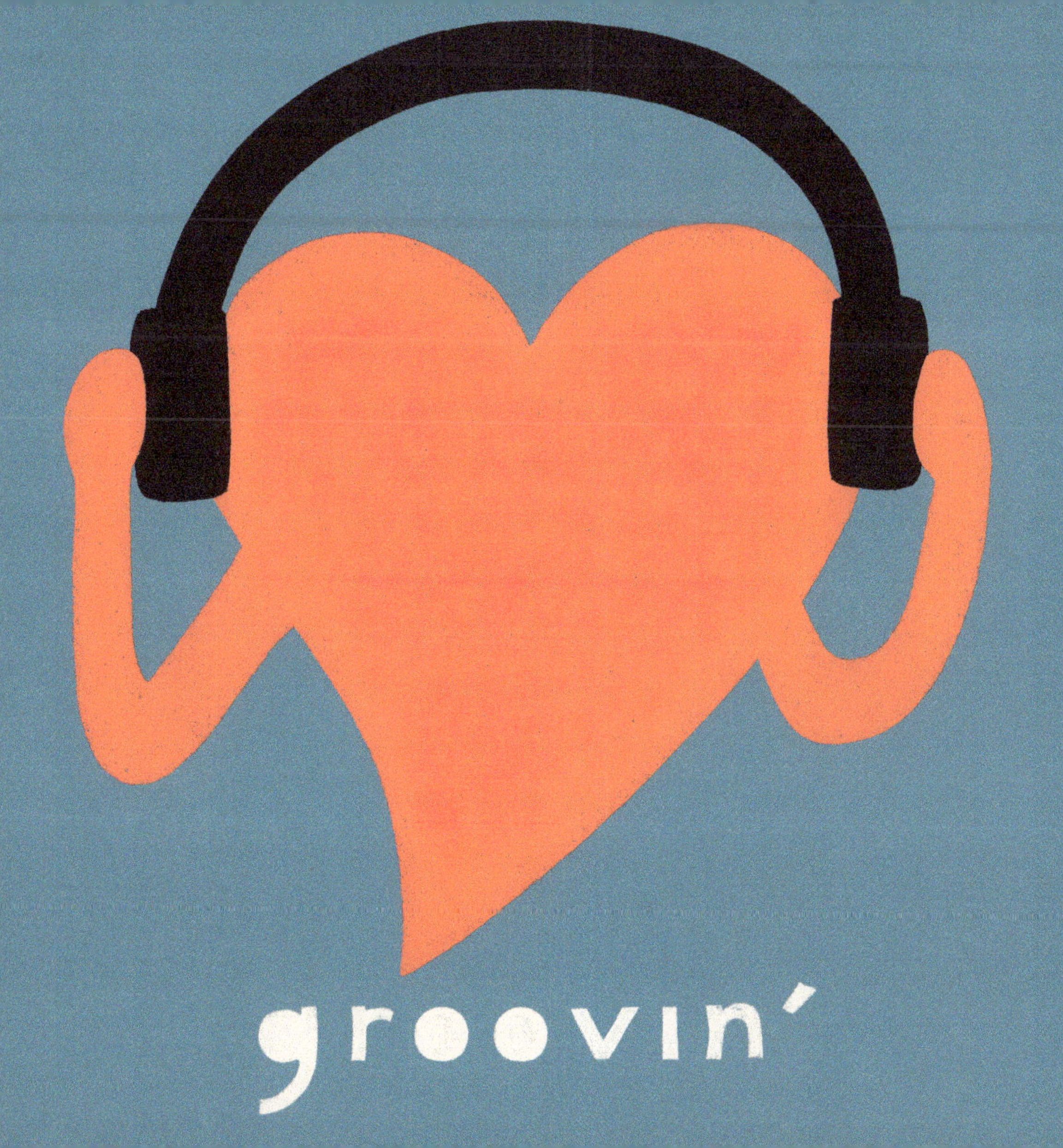
groovin'

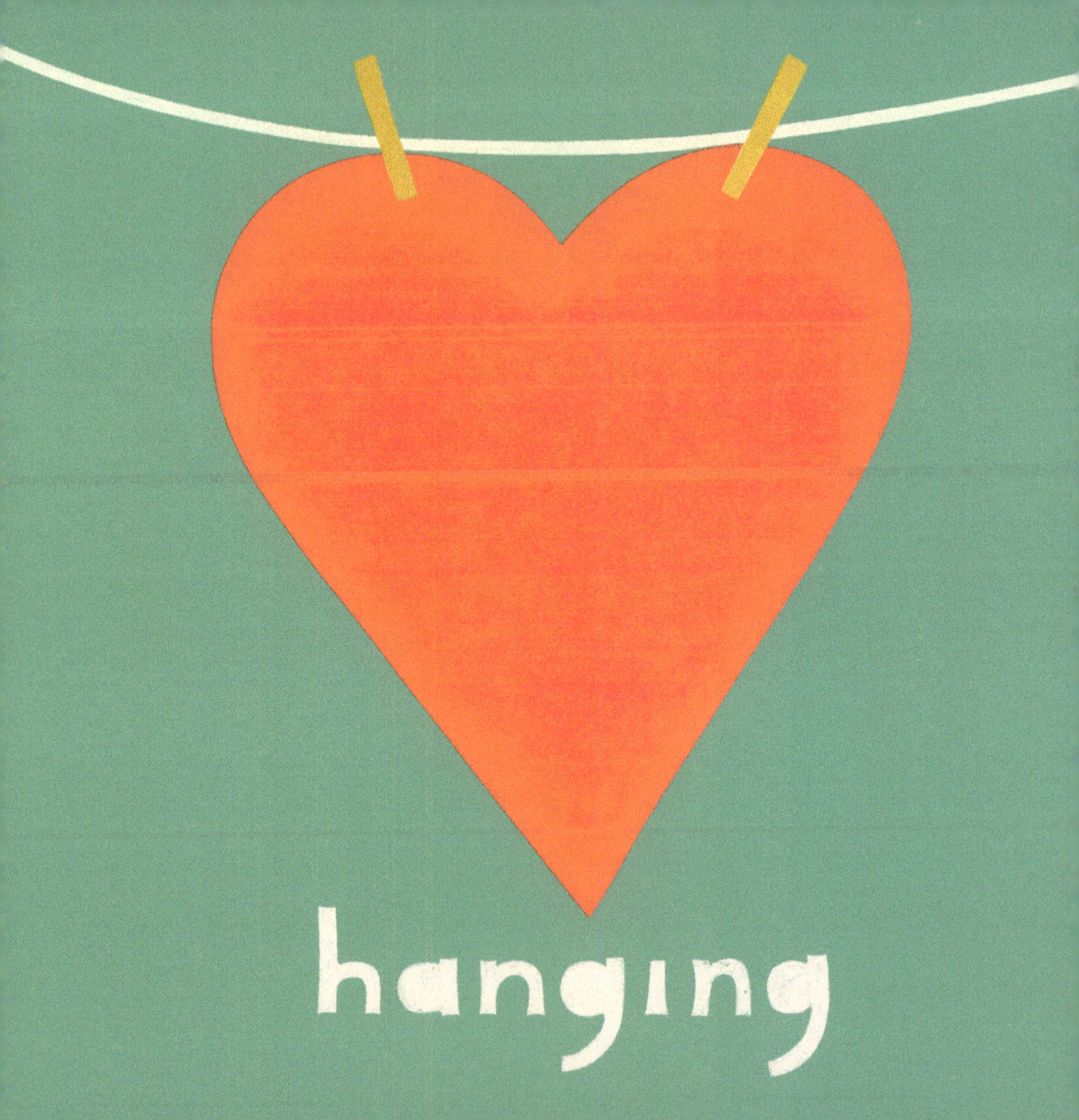

hanging

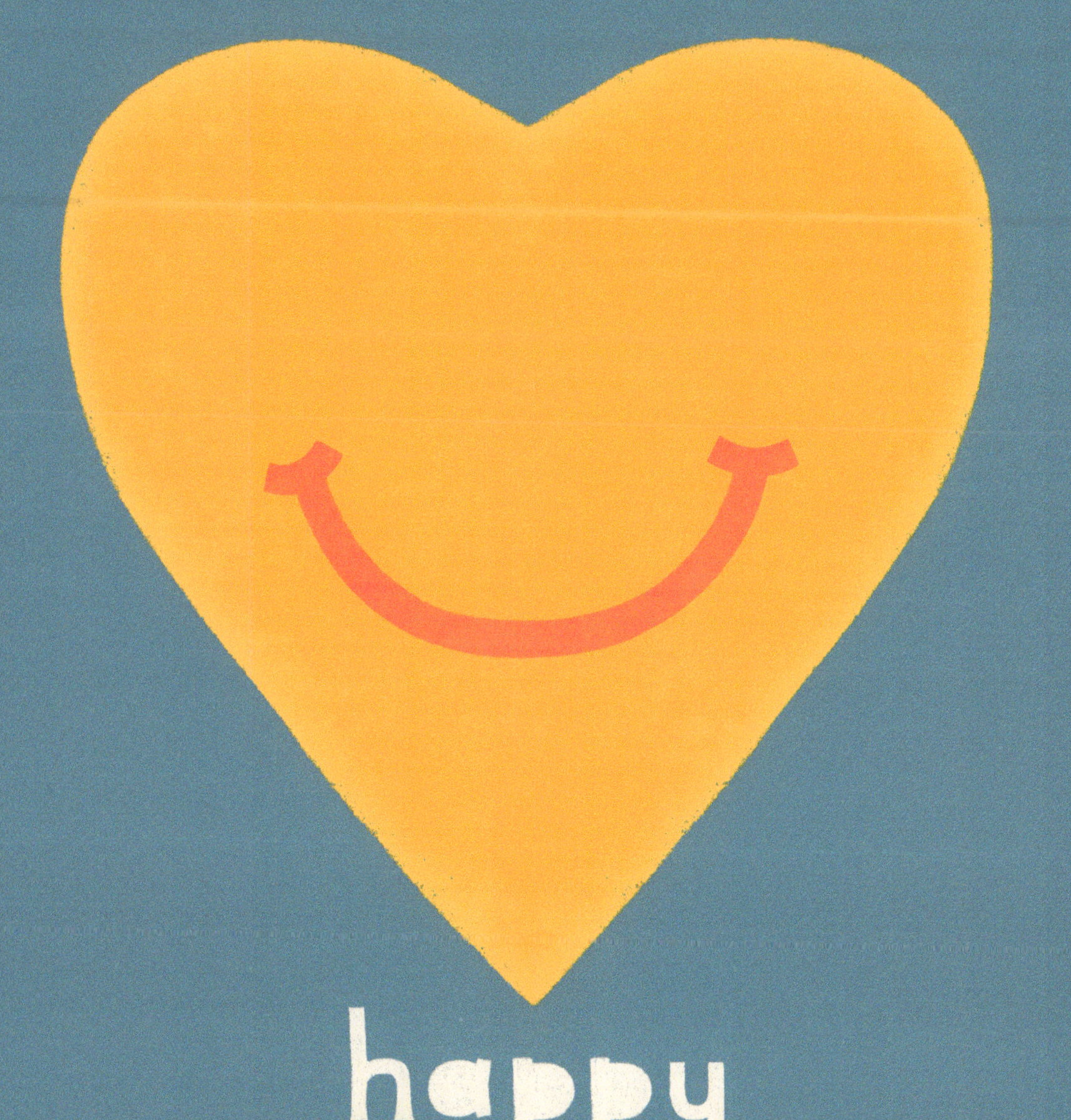

happy

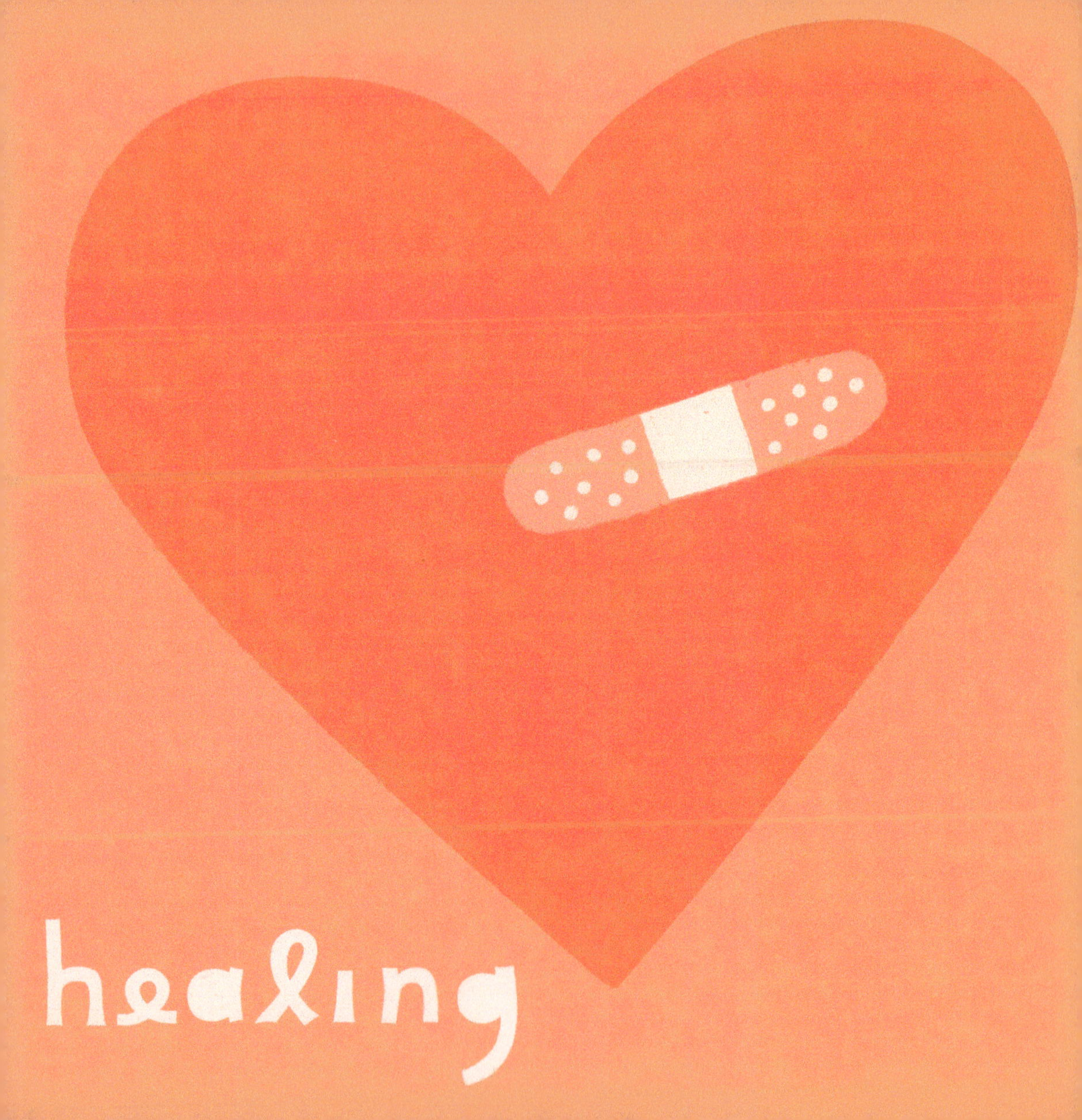
healing

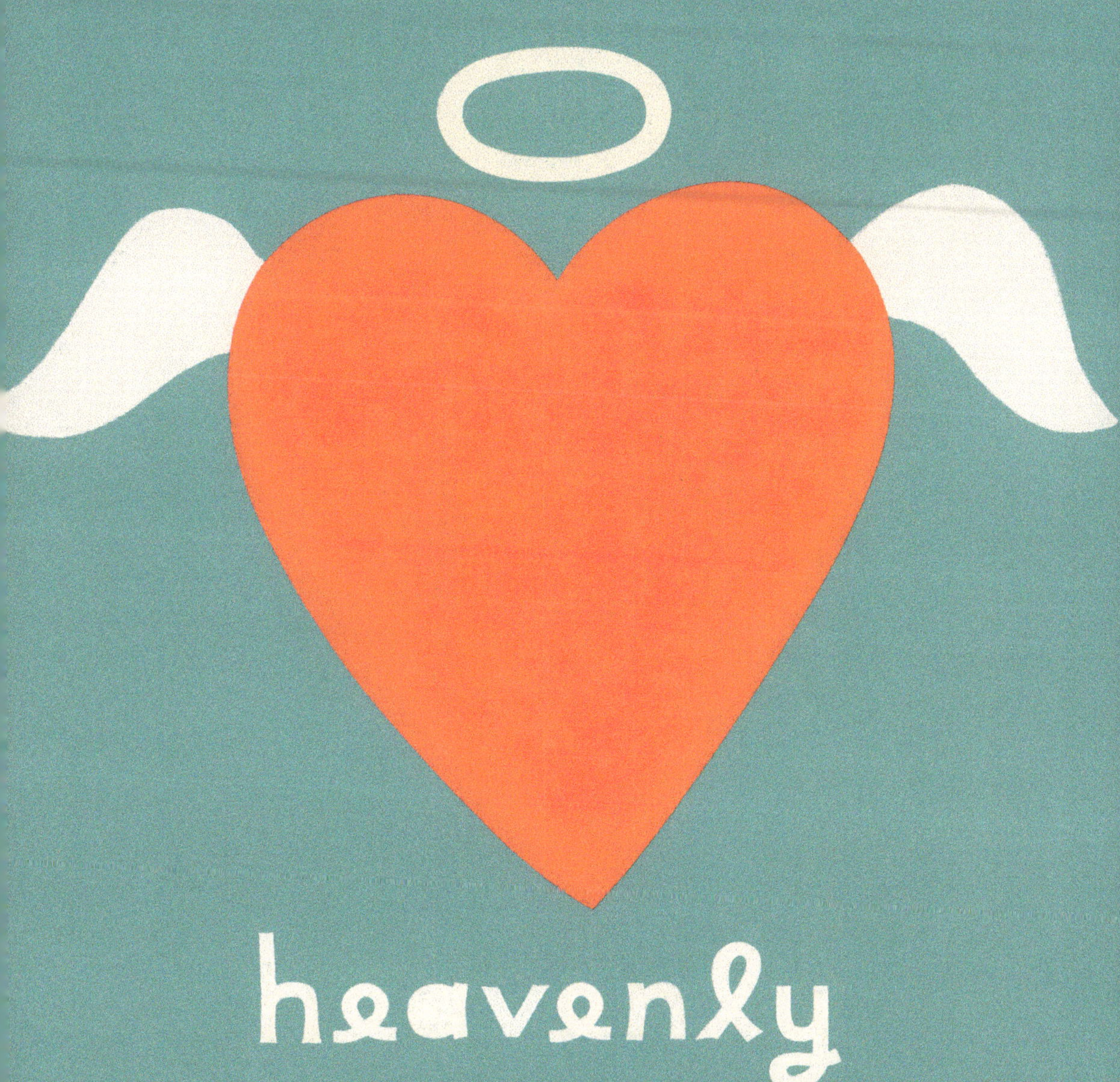
heavenly

heavy

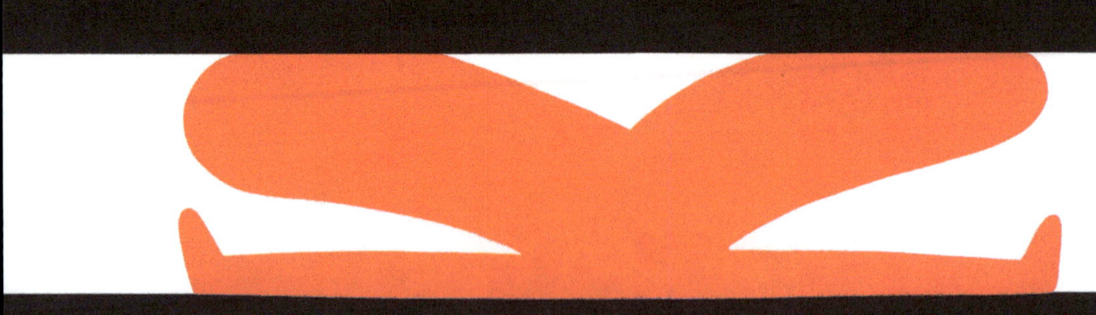

hesitant

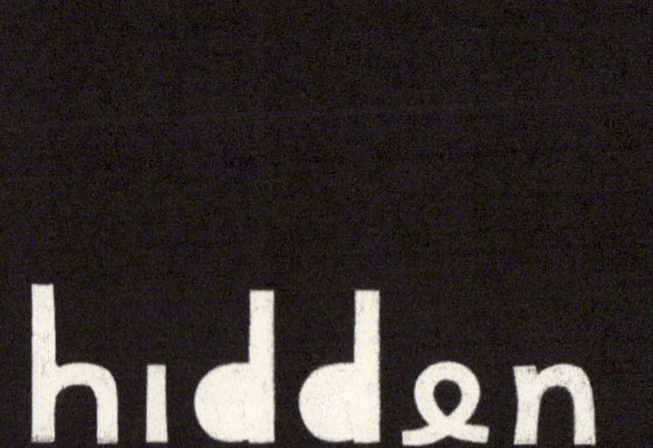

hidden

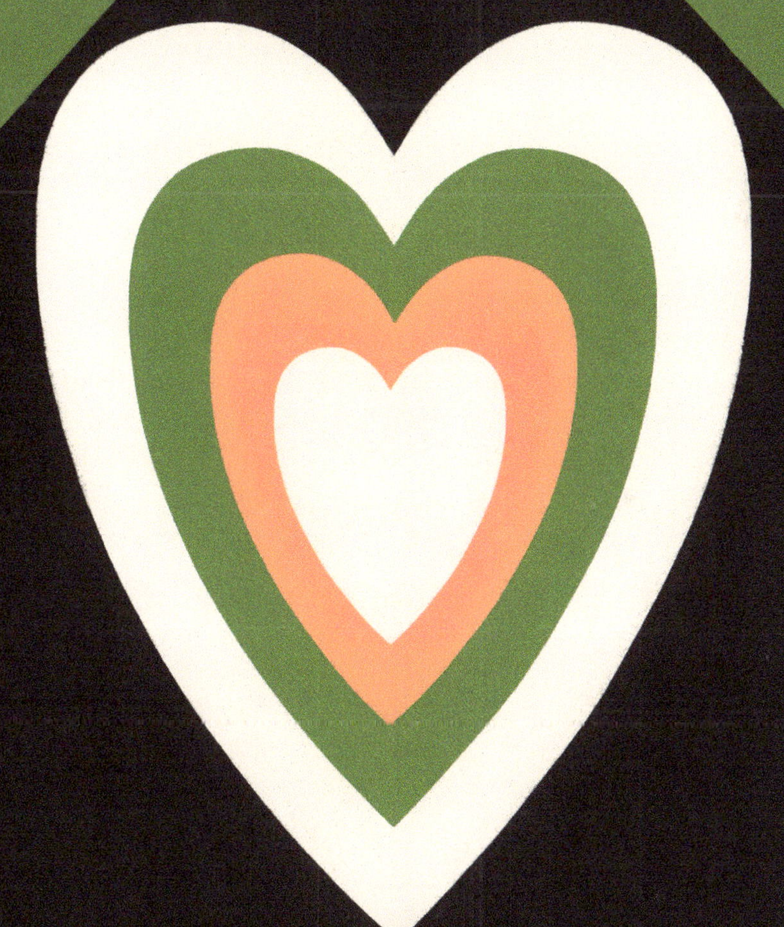

home

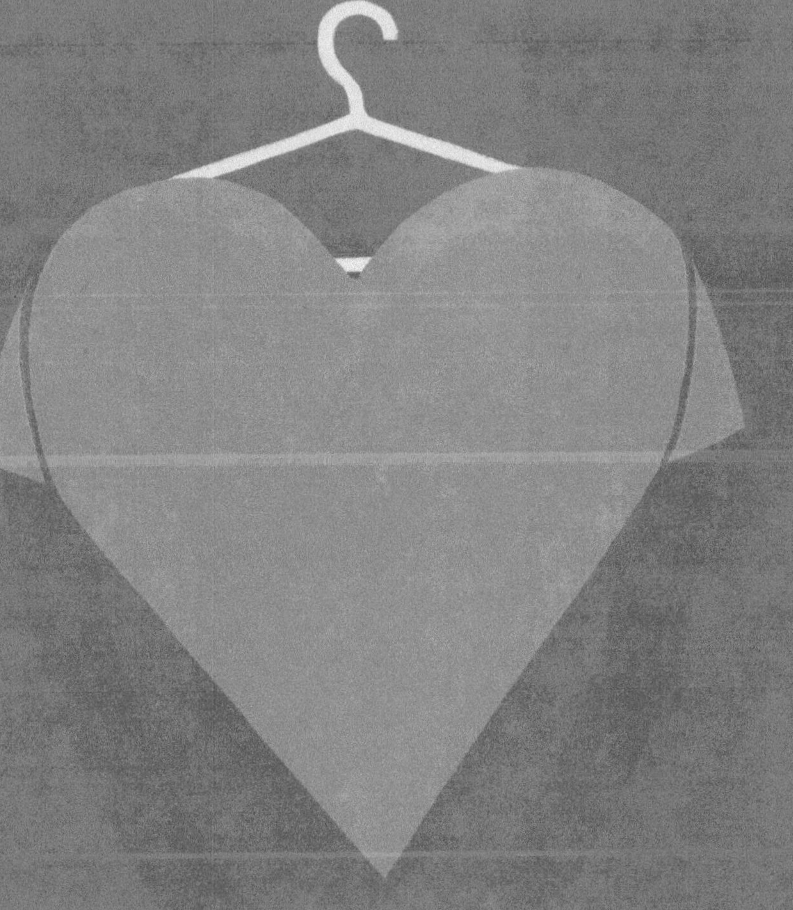
hung up

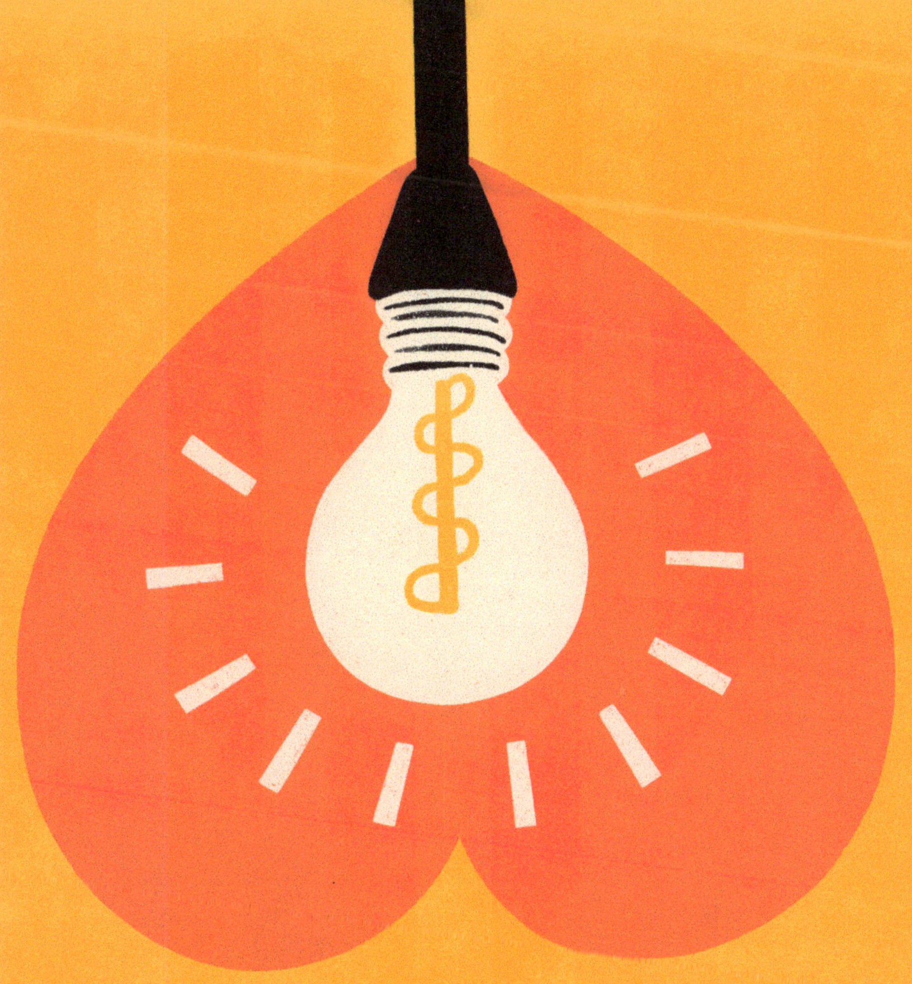
illuminate

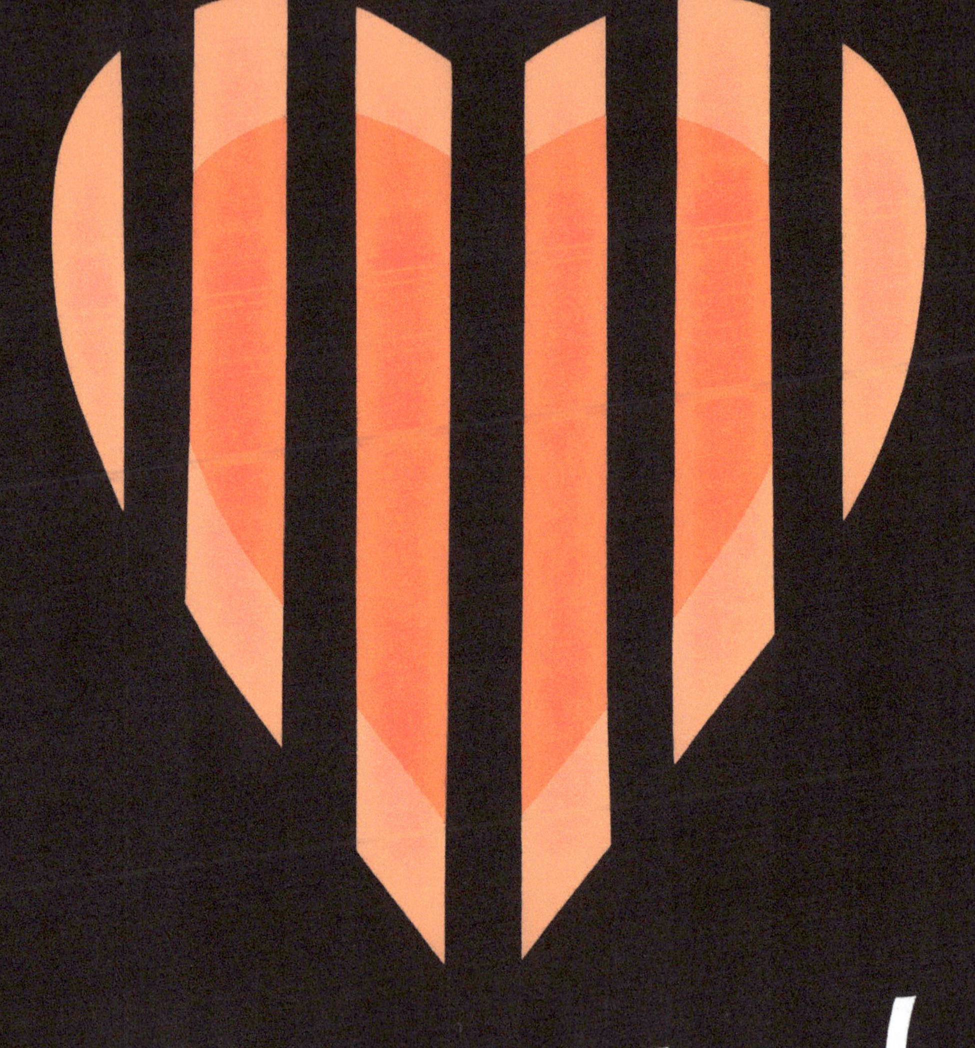

imprisioned

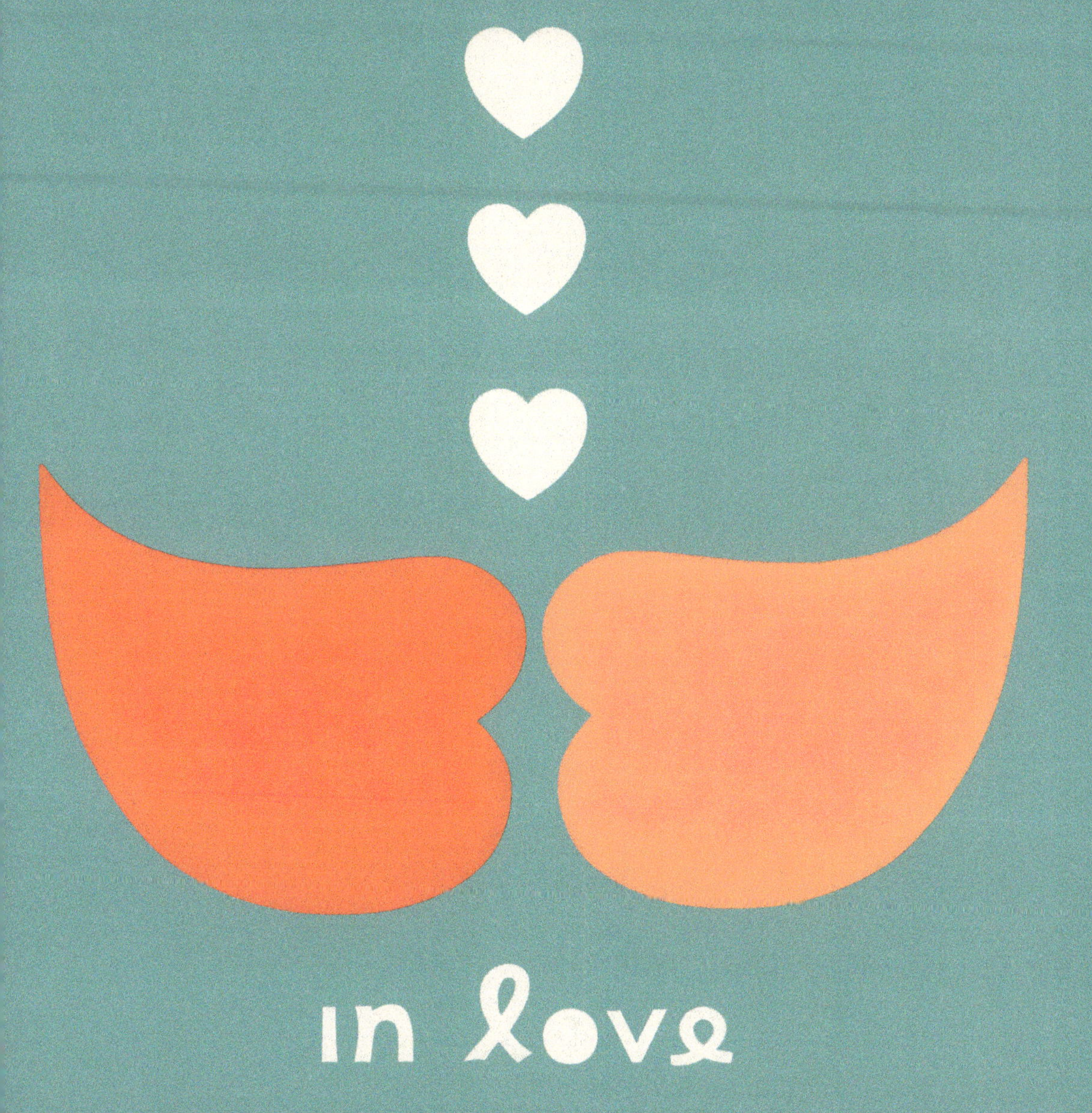
in love

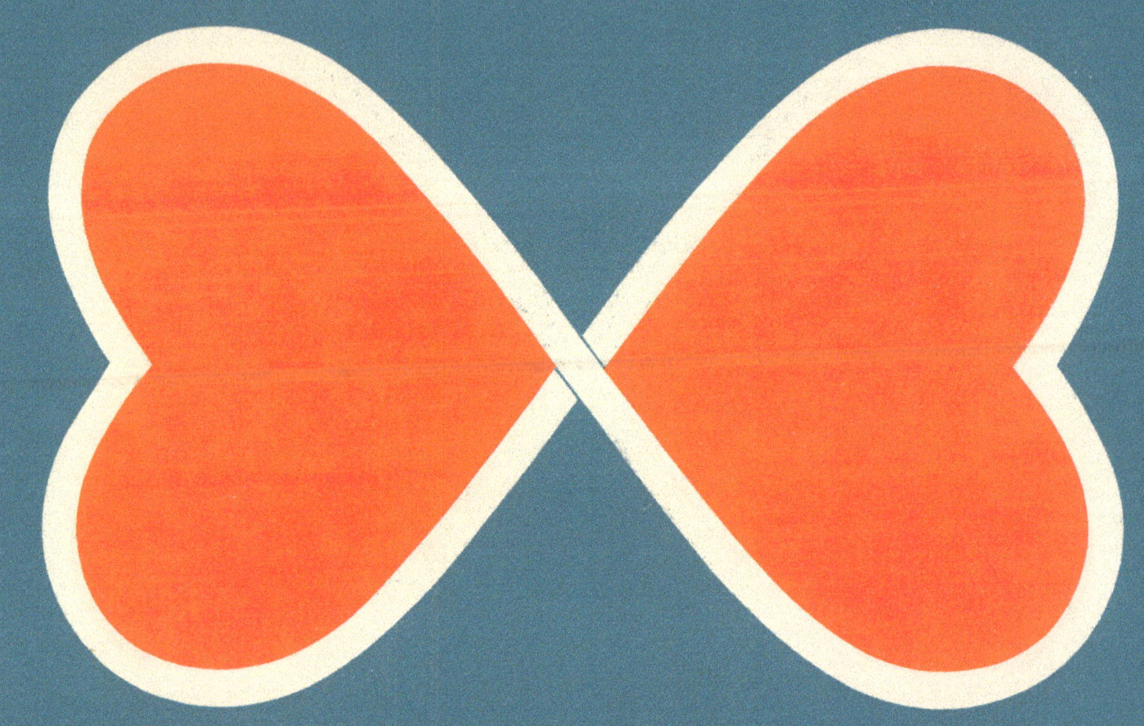

infinite

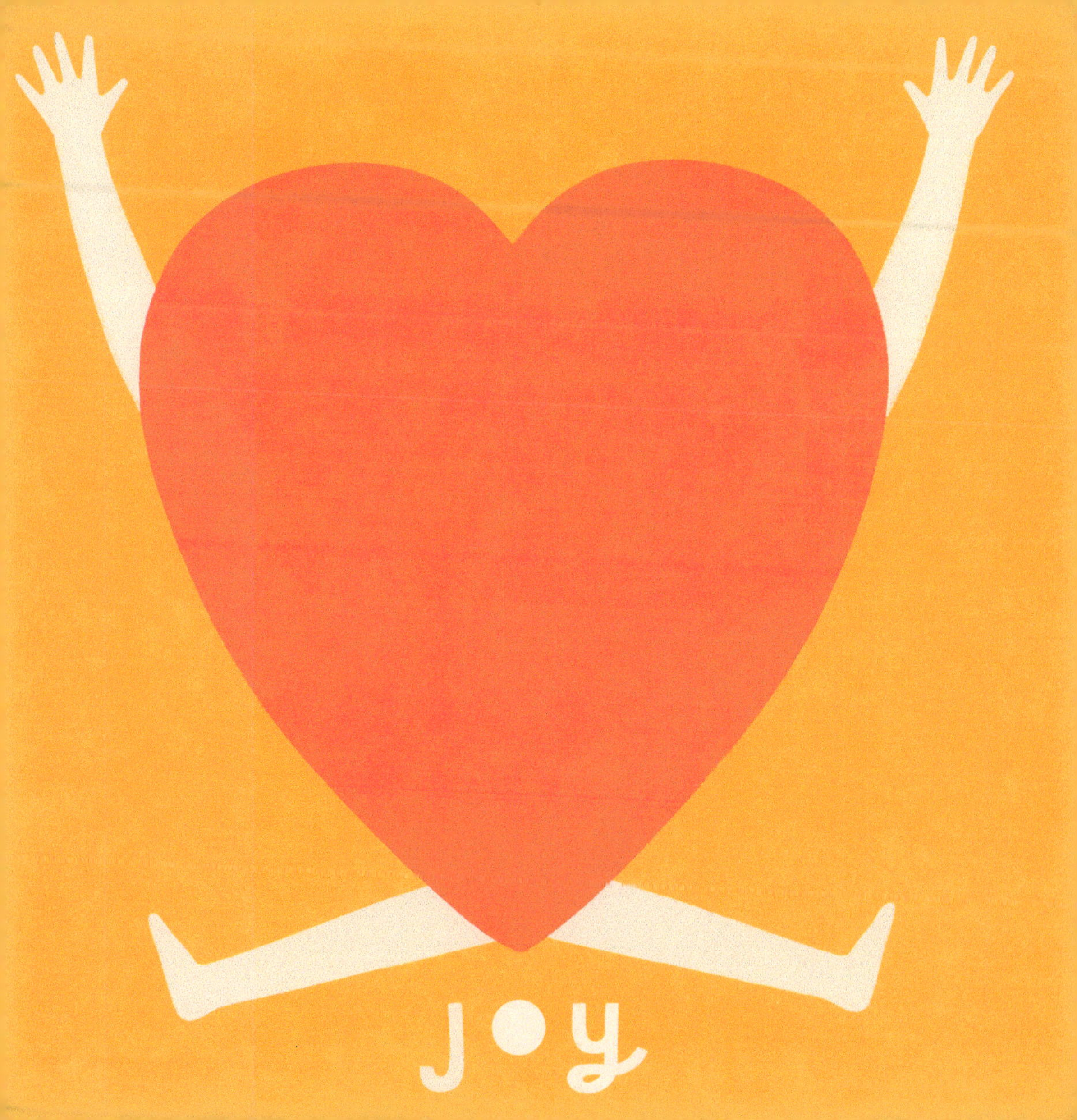
JOY

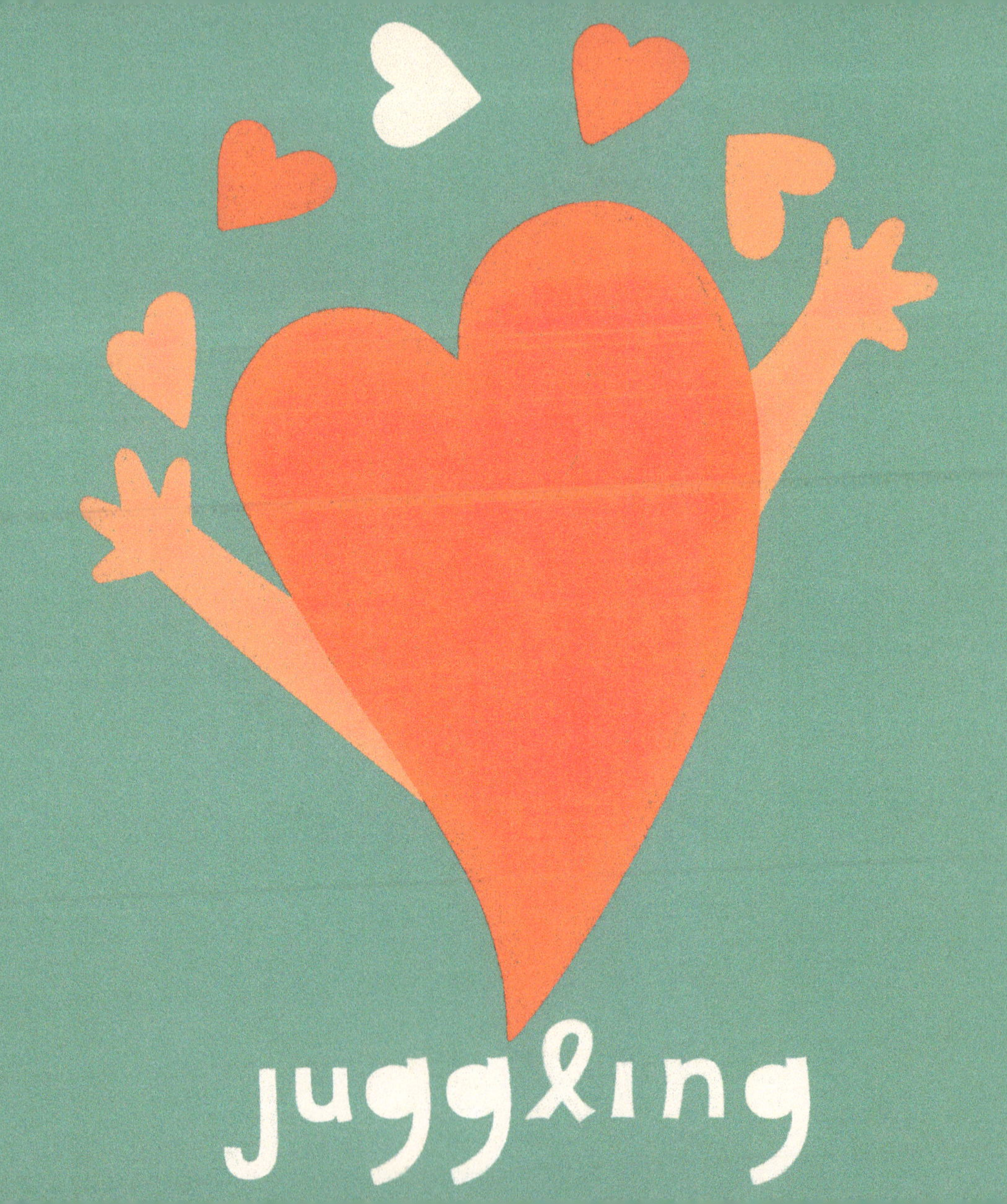

juggling

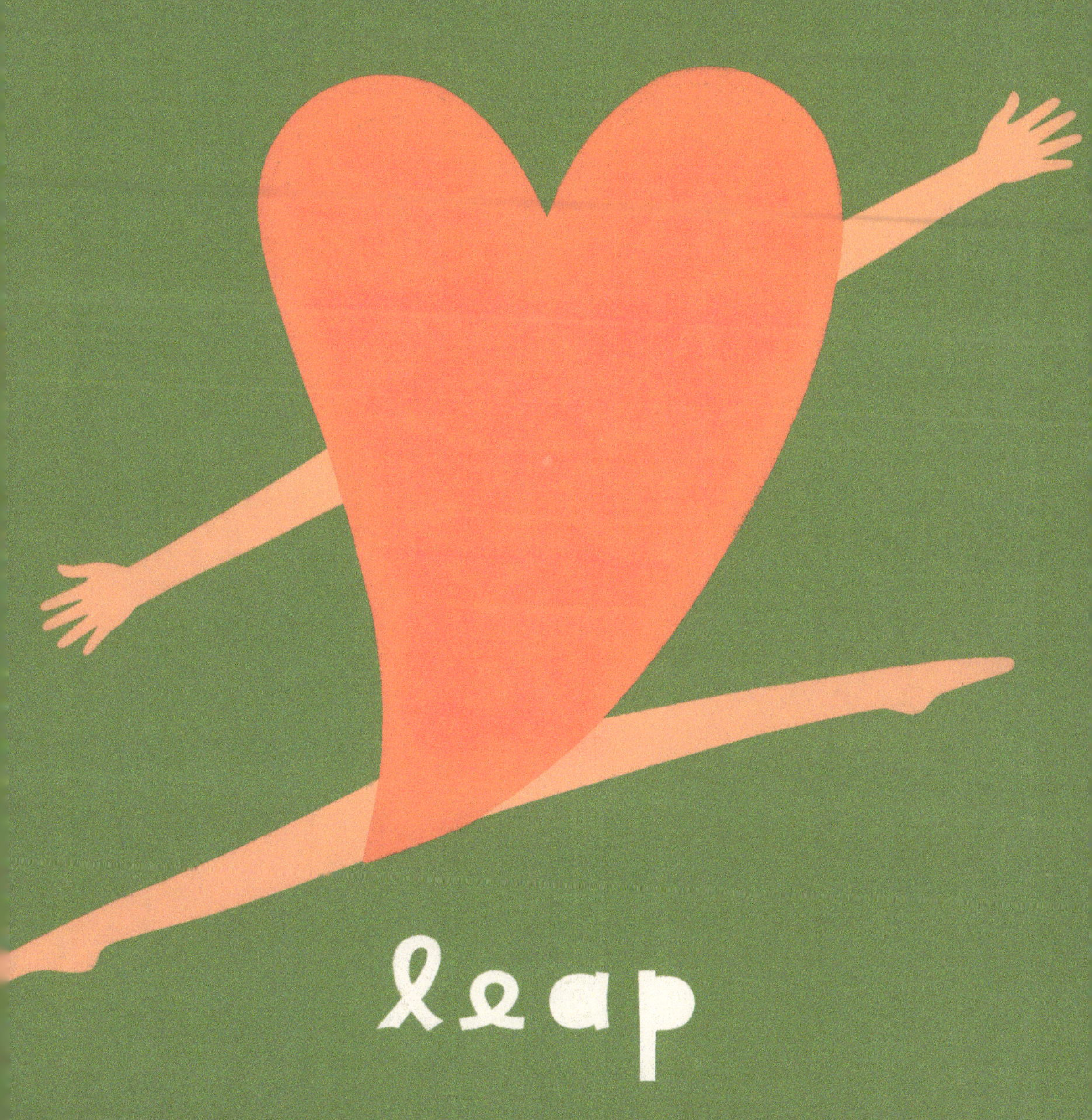

leap

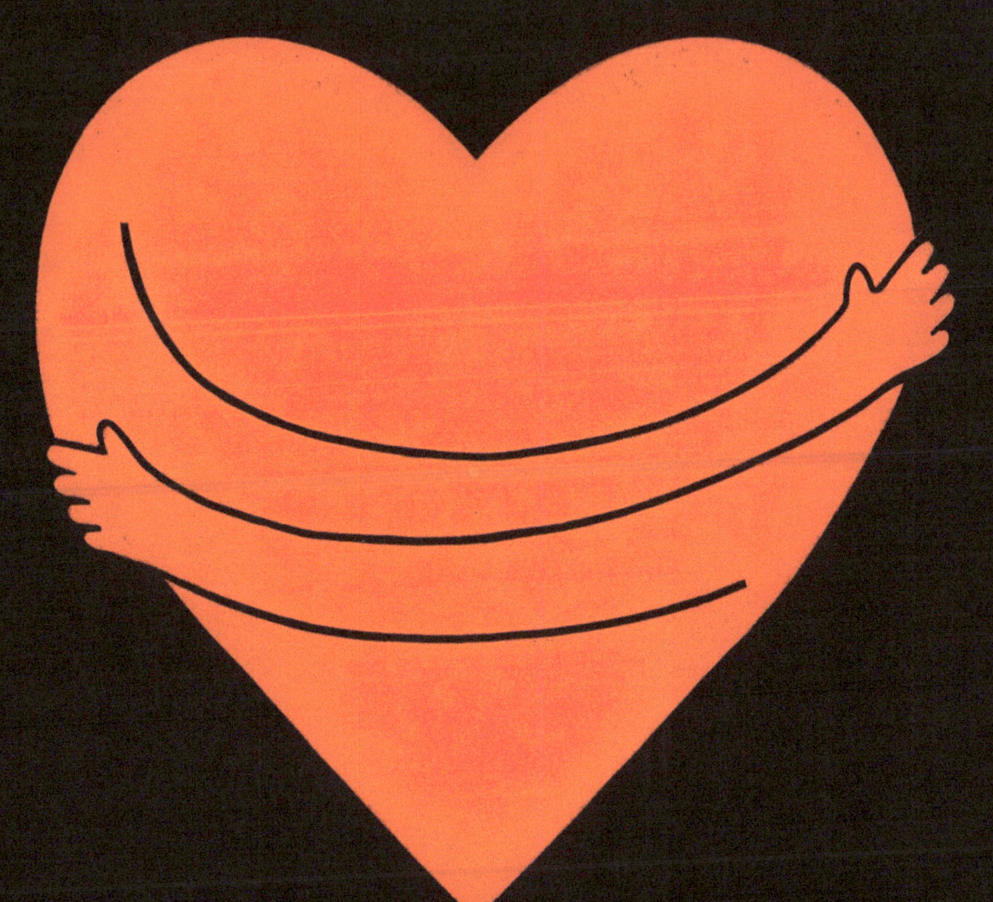

loving

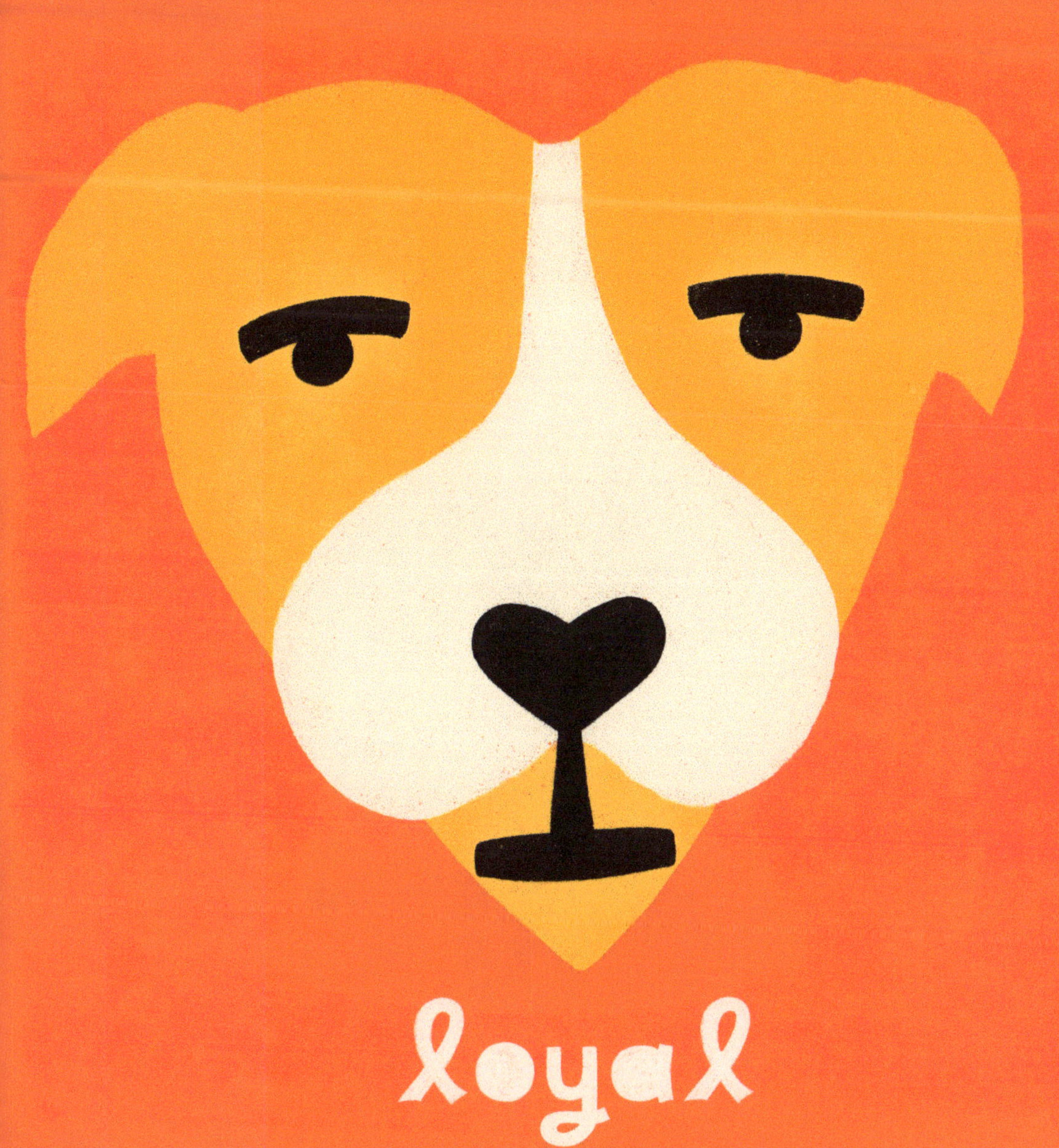
loyal

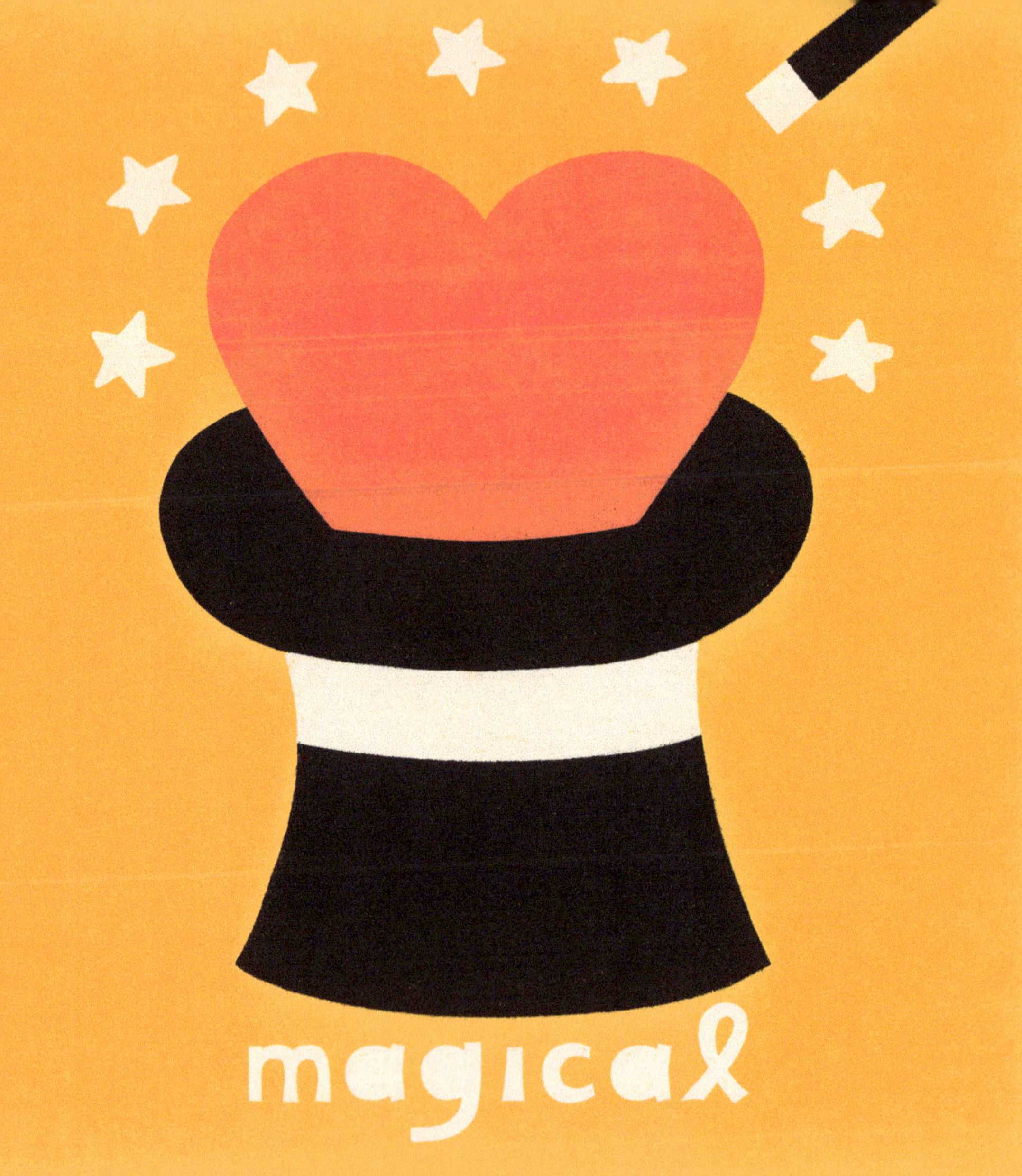

magical

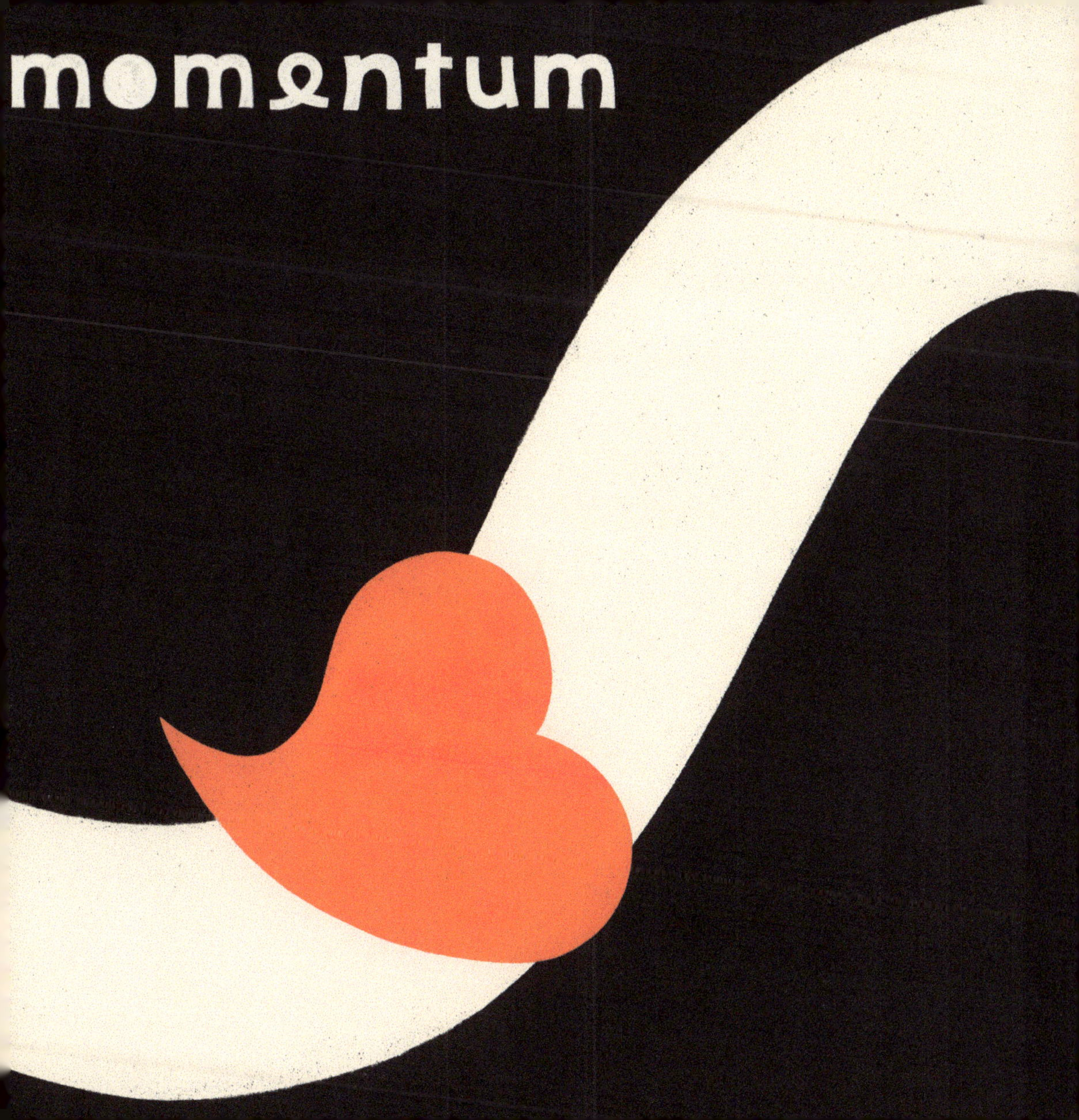
momentum

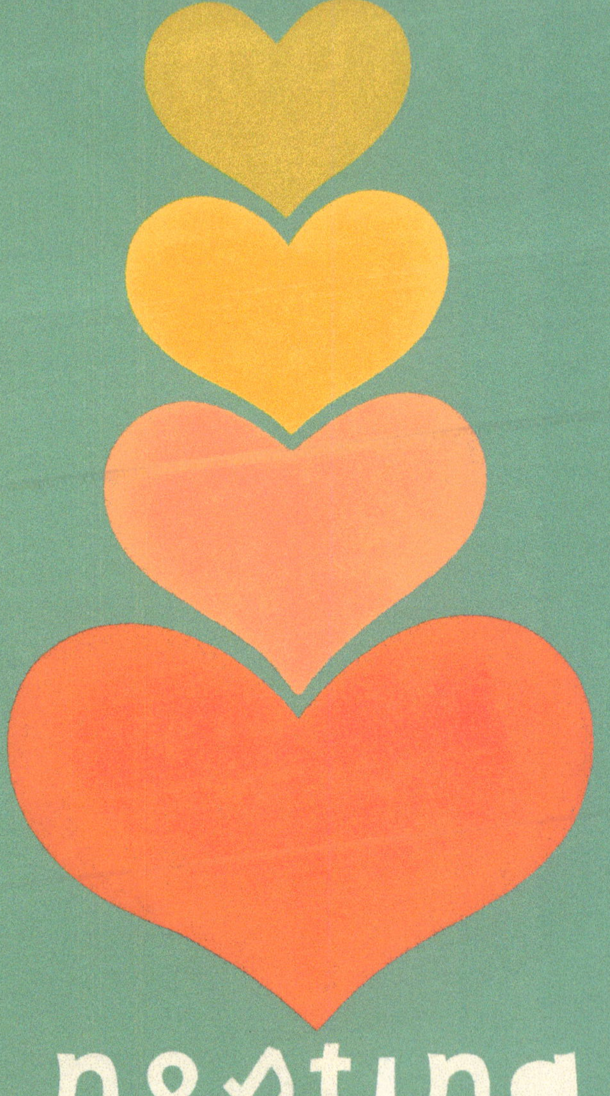

nesting

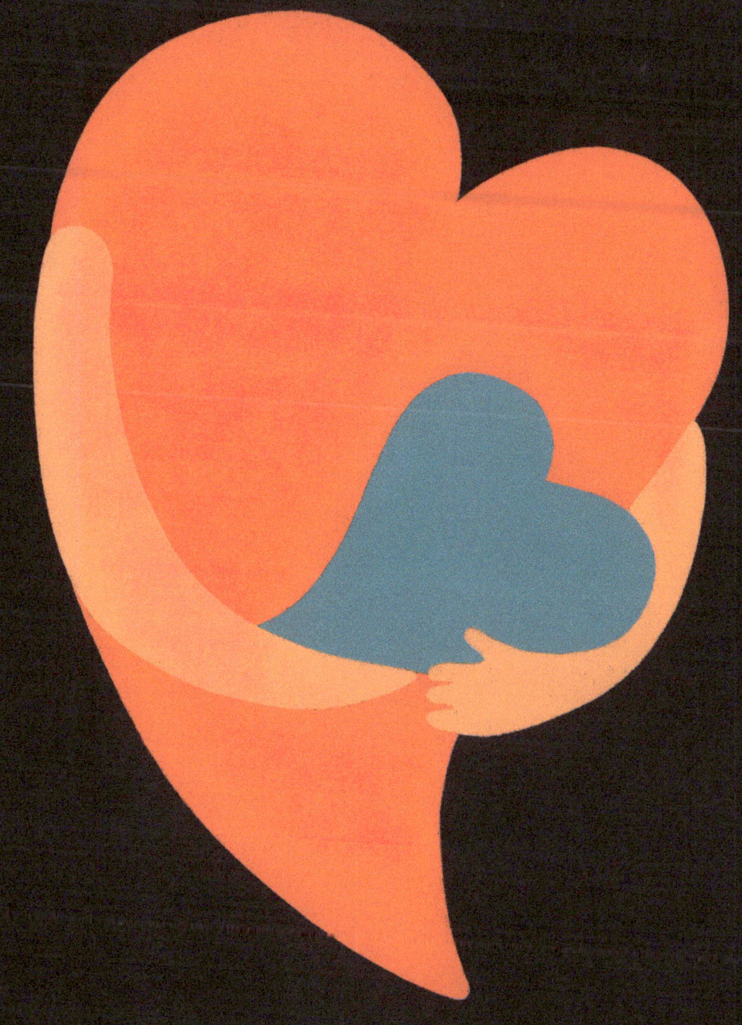

nurture

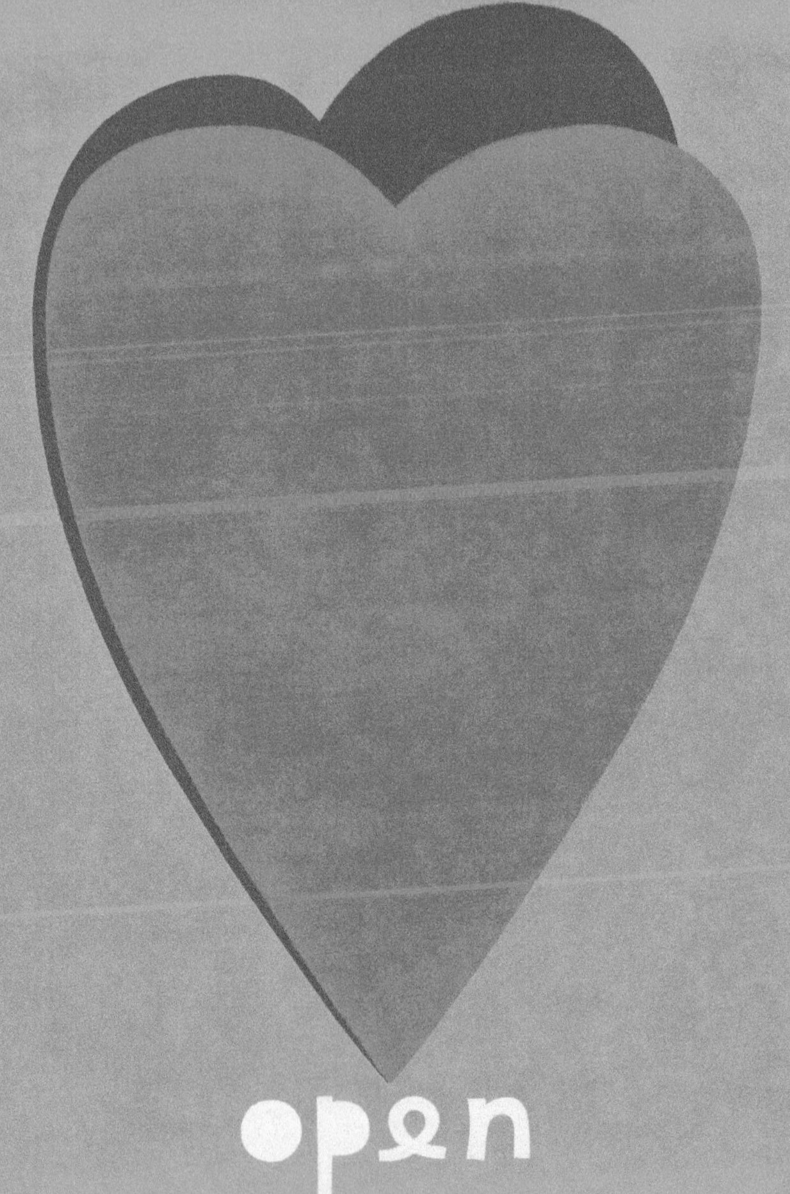

open

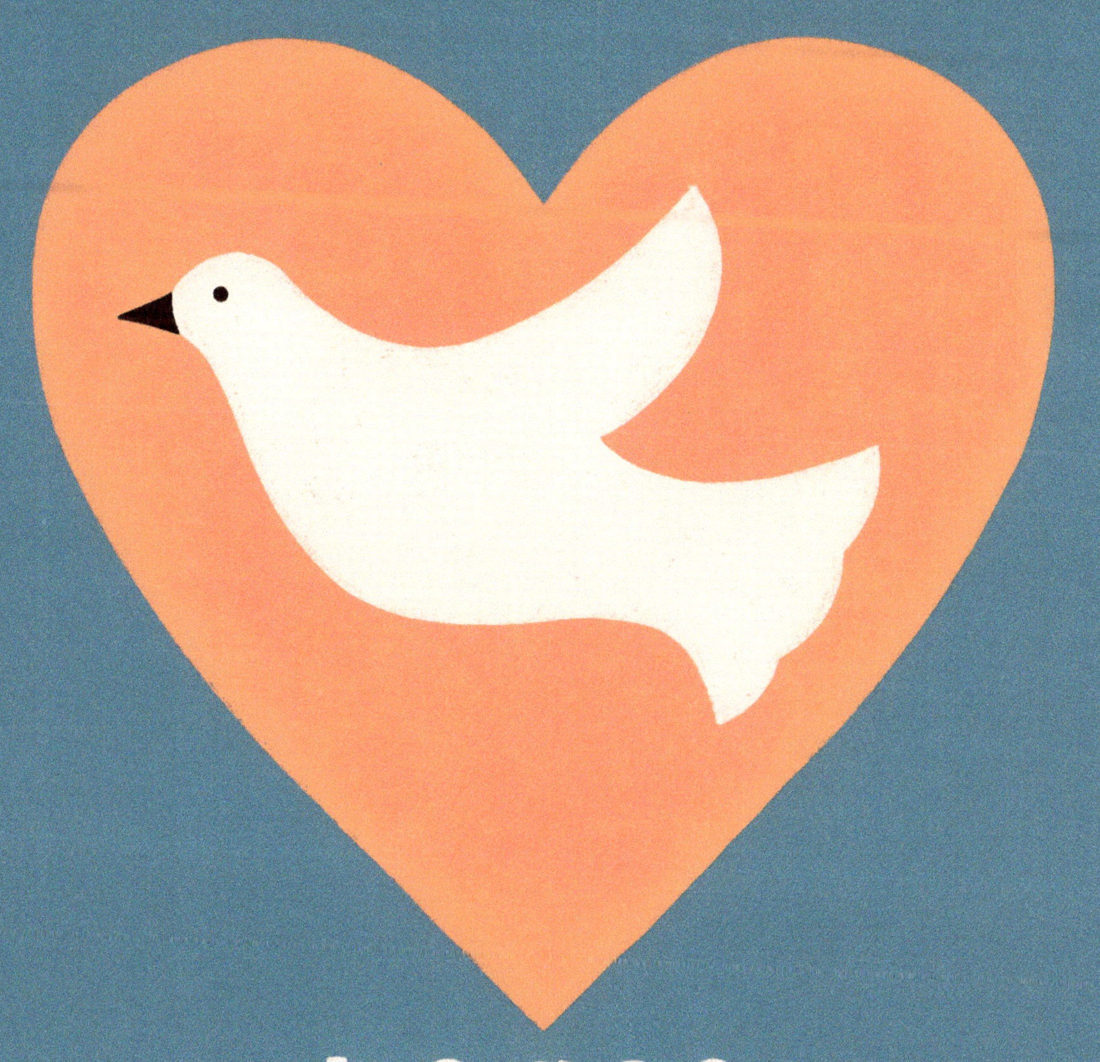

peace

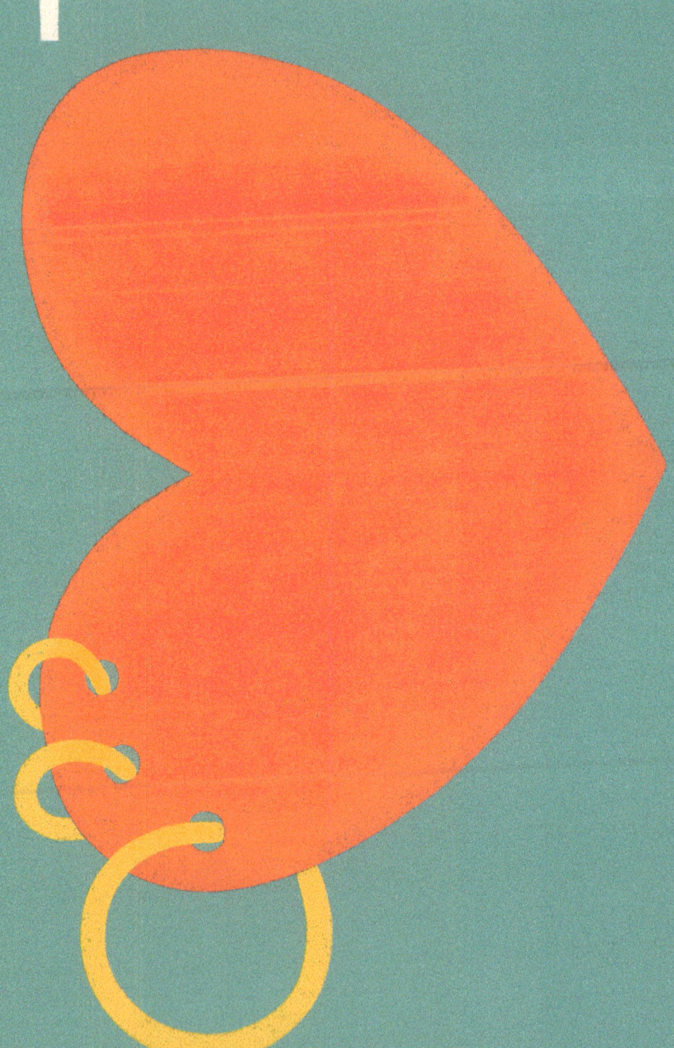

pierced

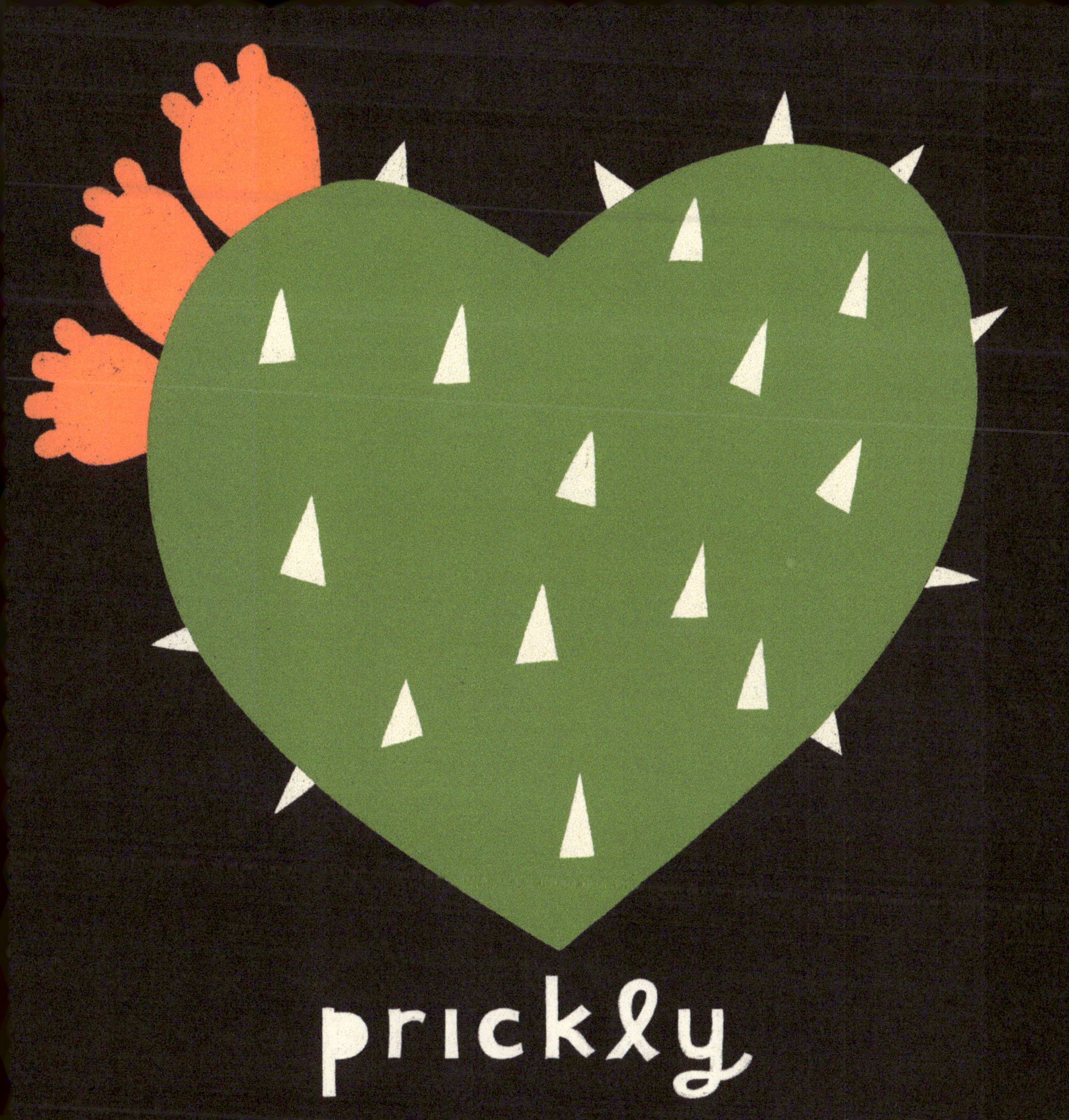
prickly

protect

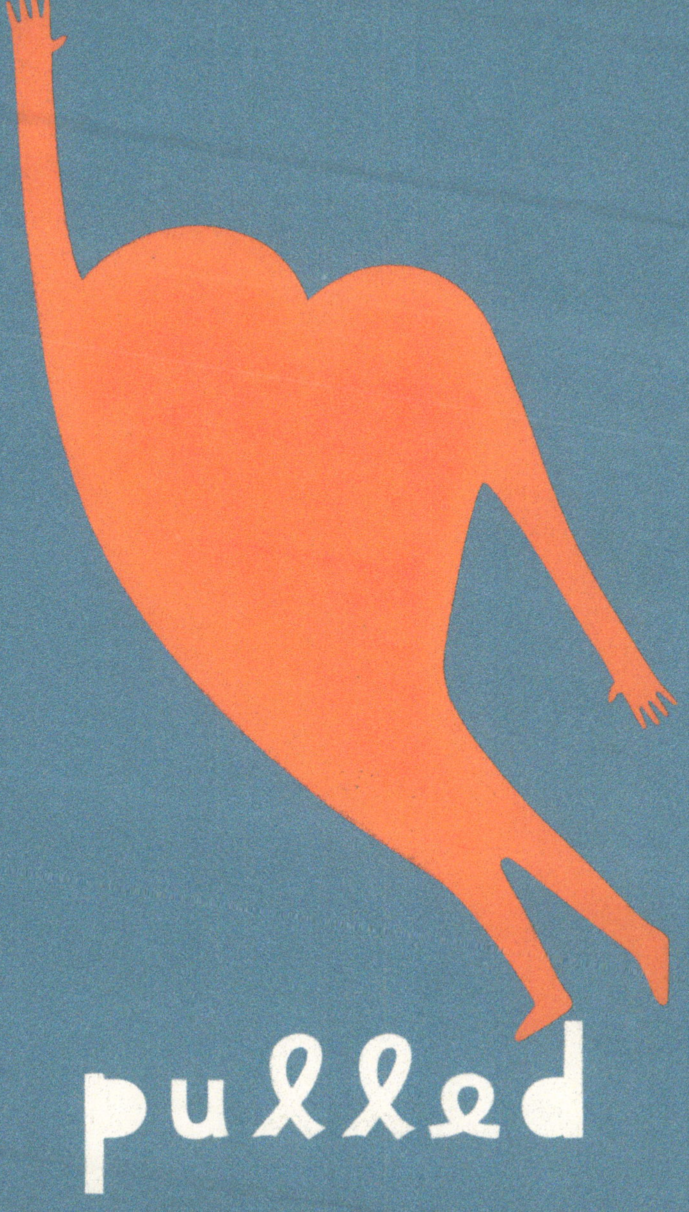

pulled

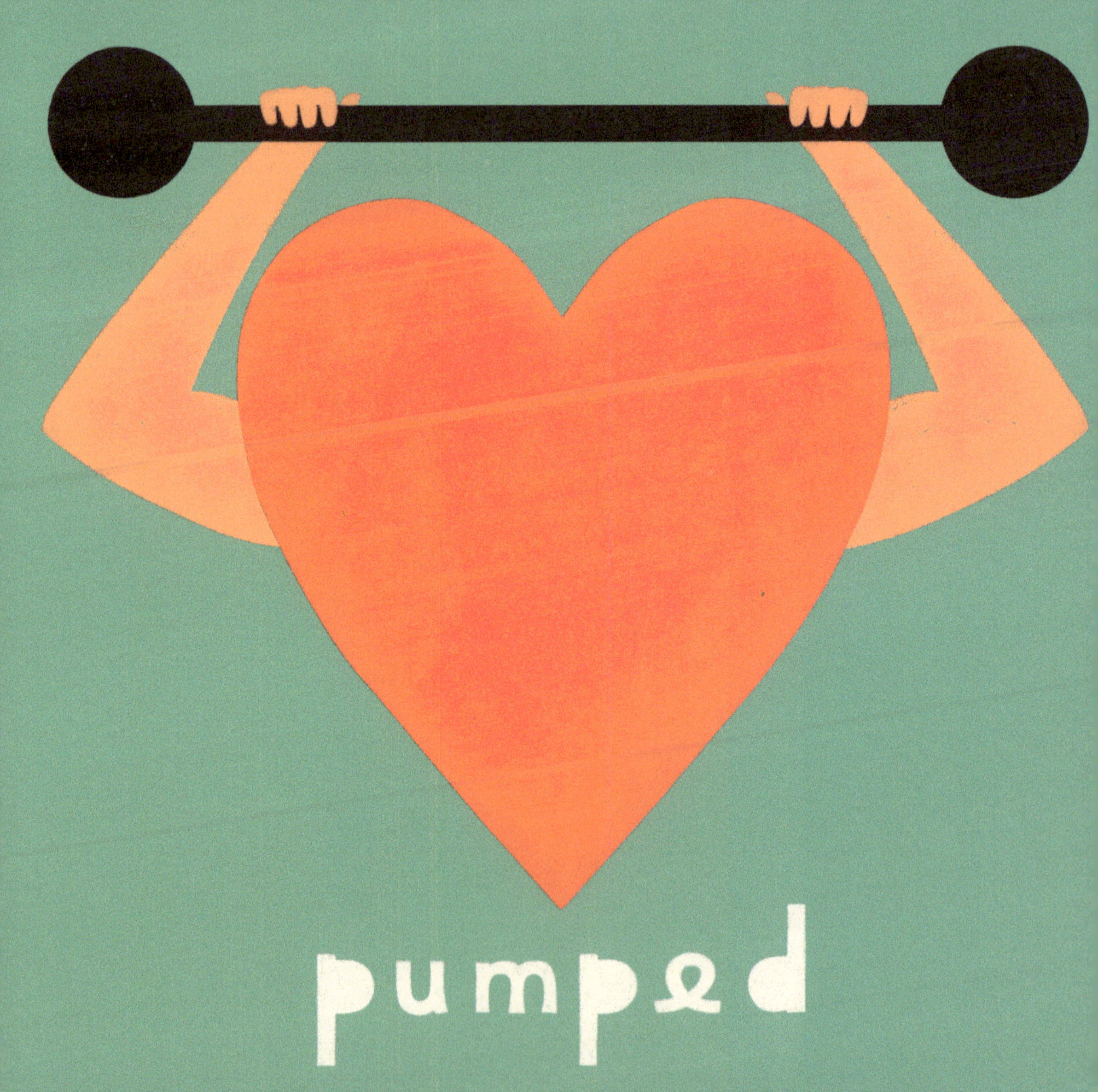
pumped

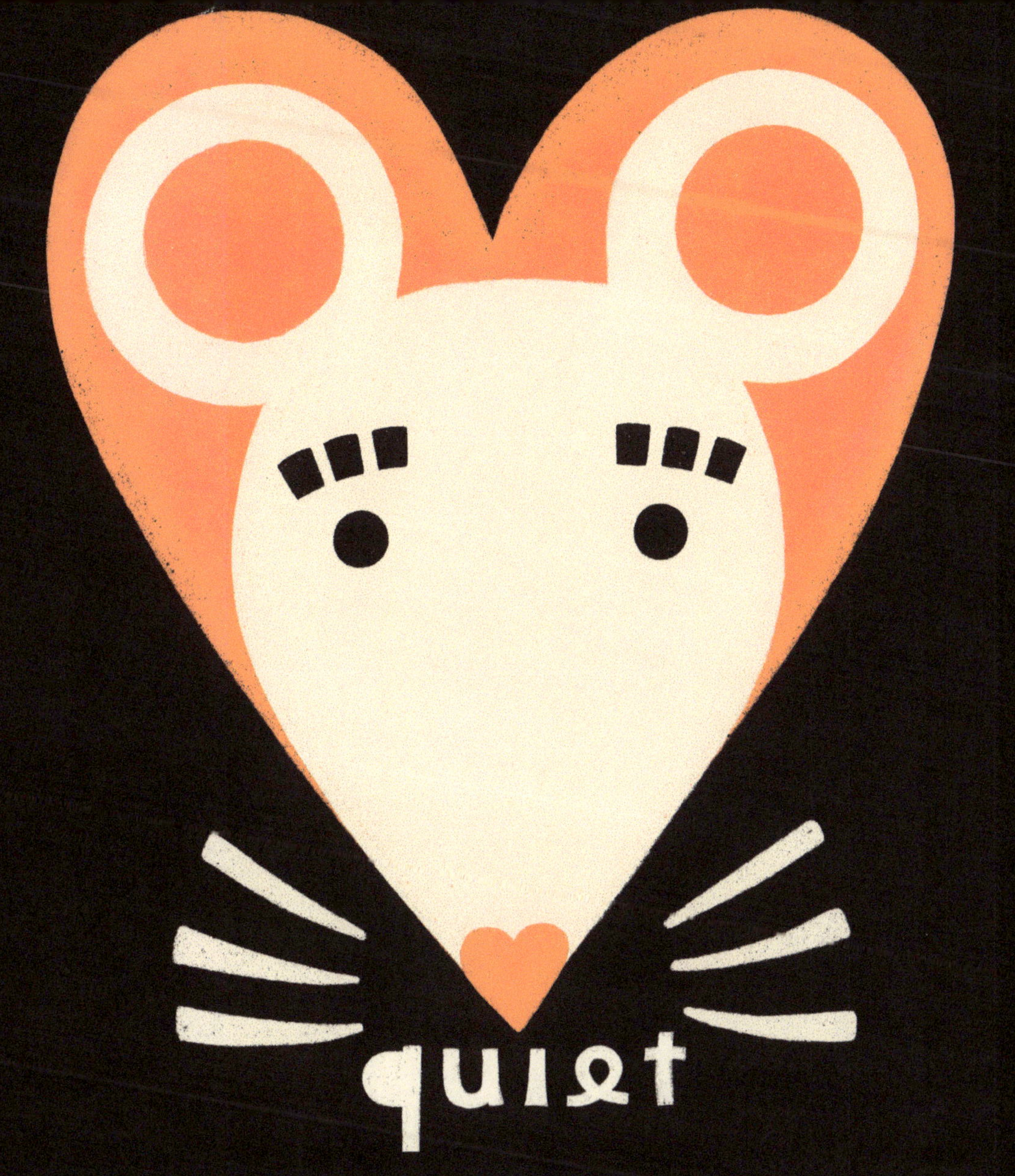
quiet

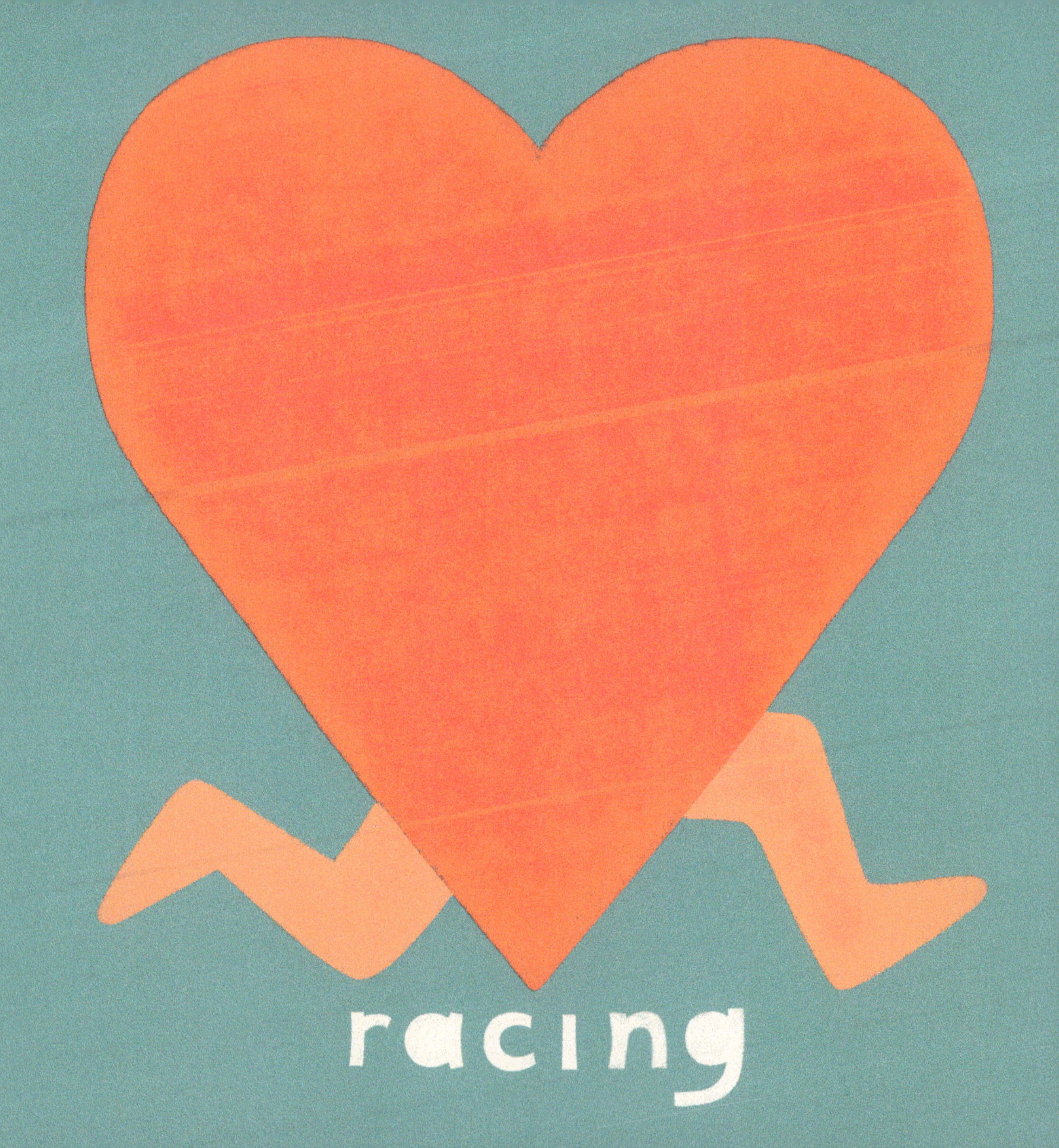

racing

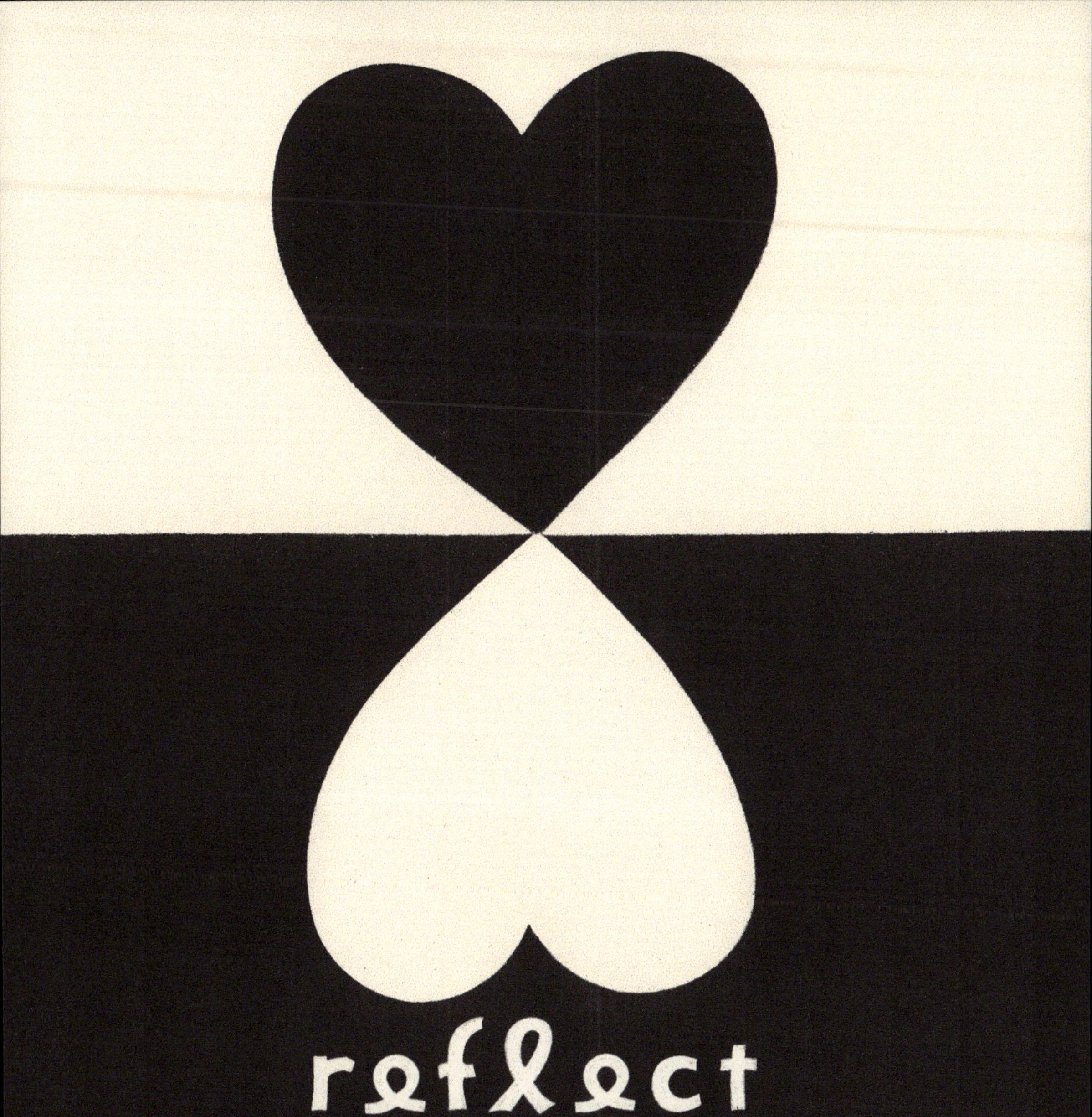

reflect

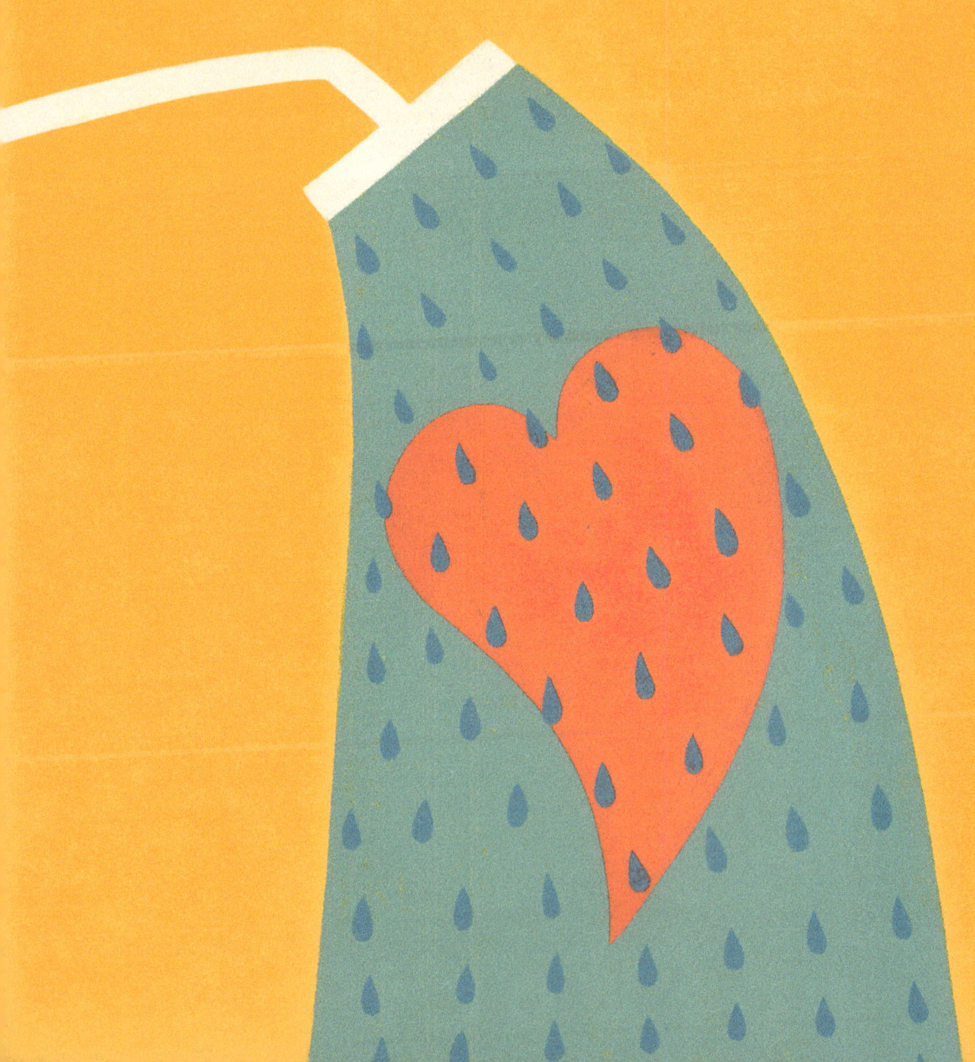
refresh

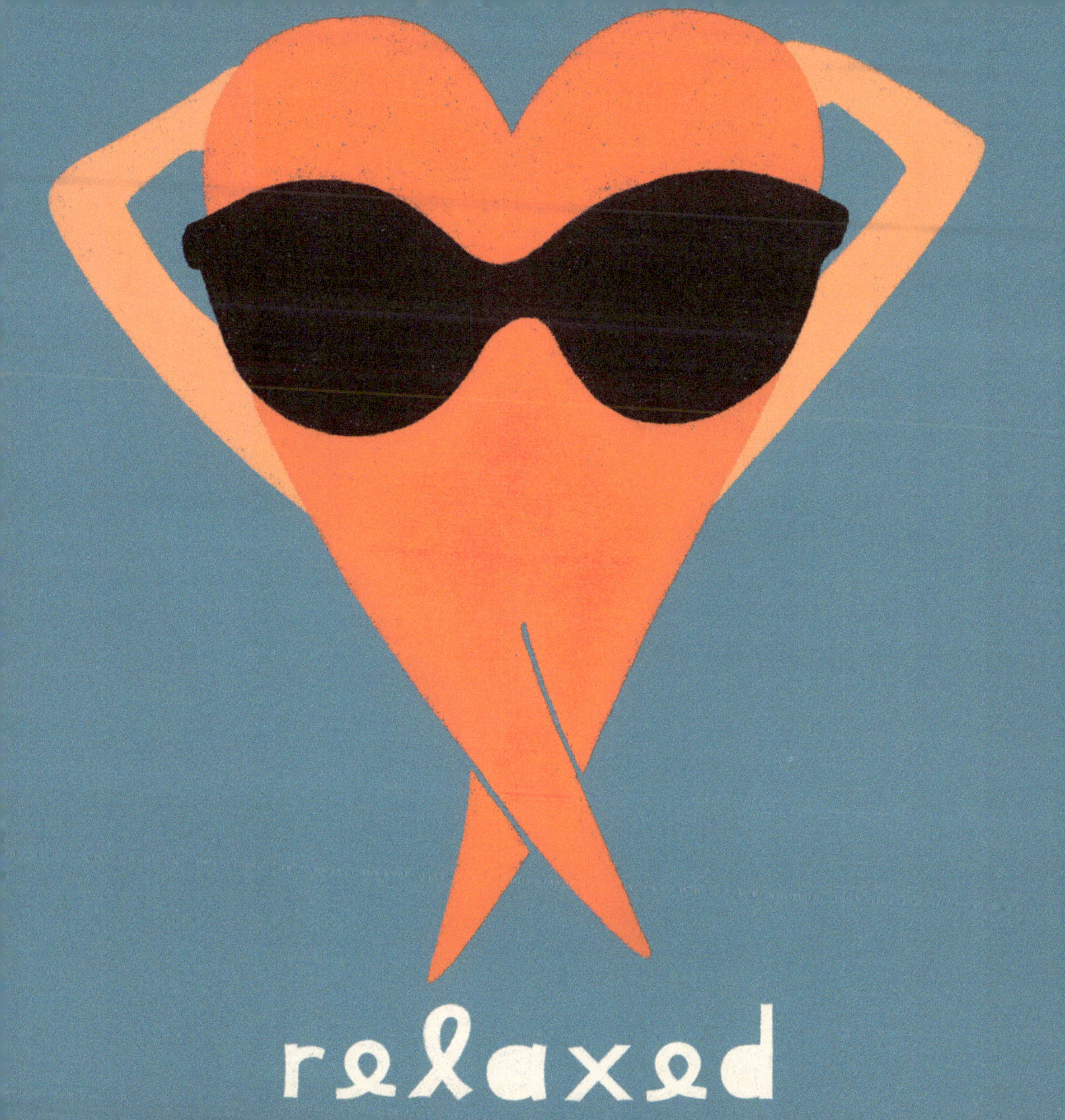
relaxed

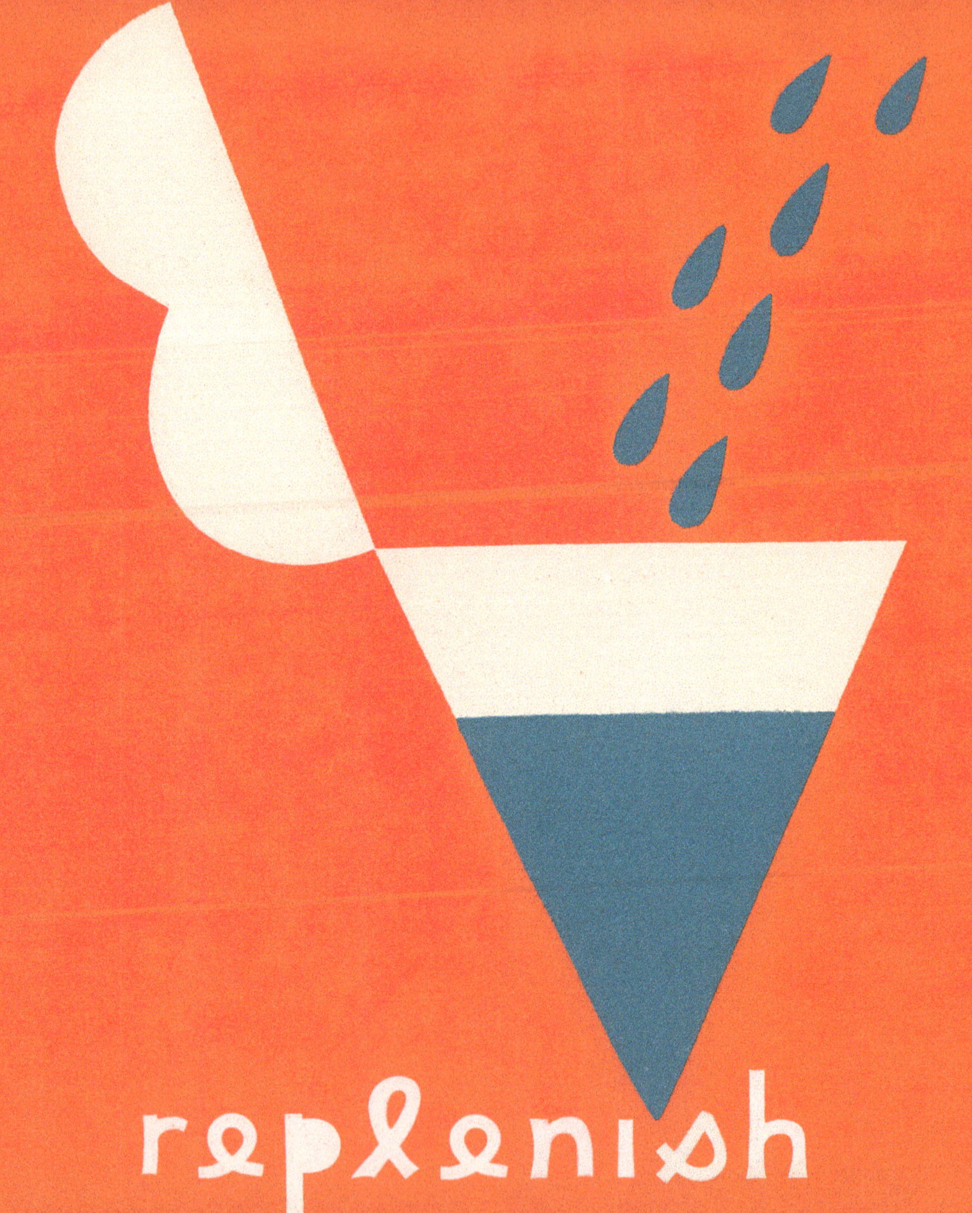

replenish

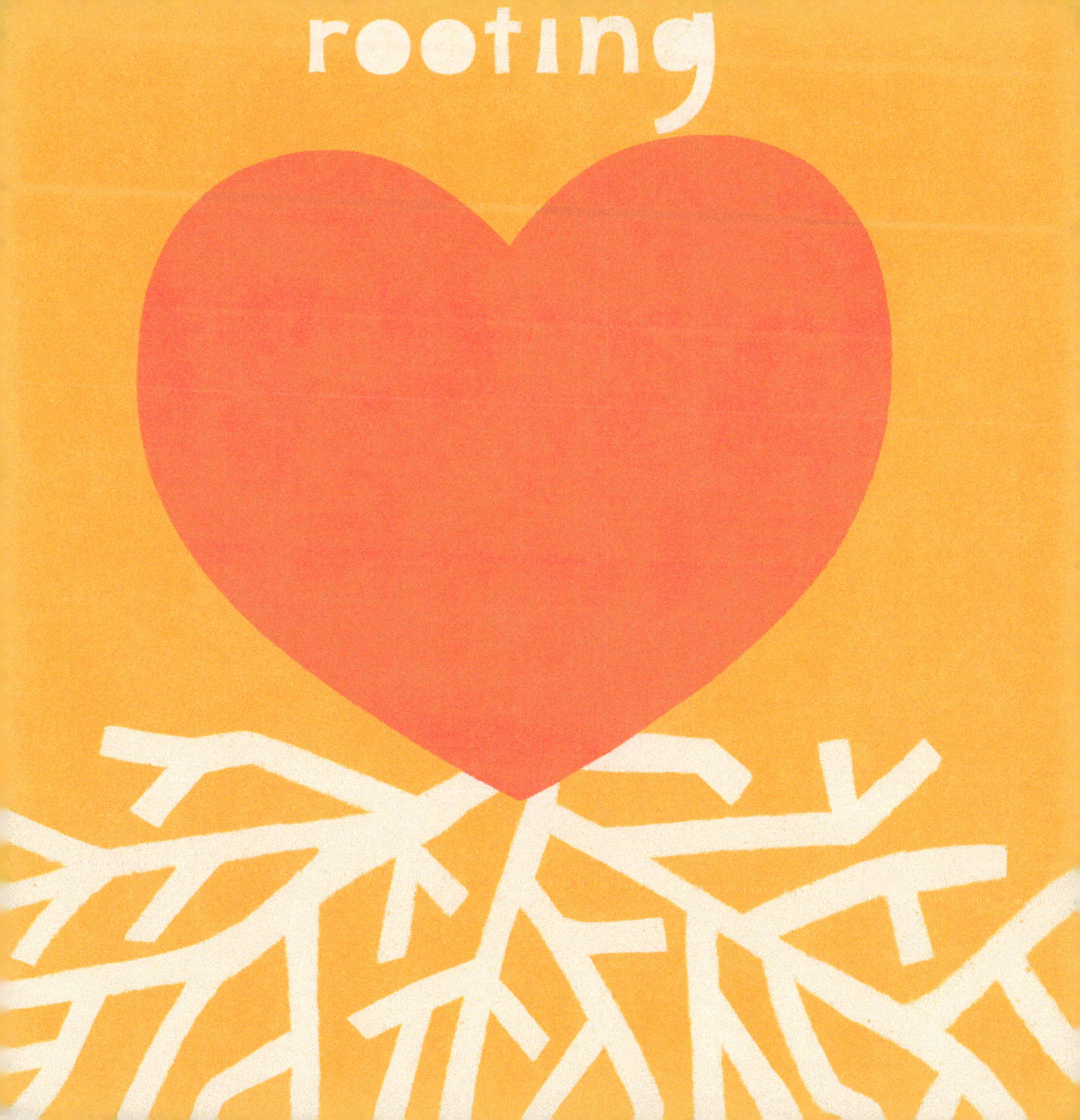
rooting

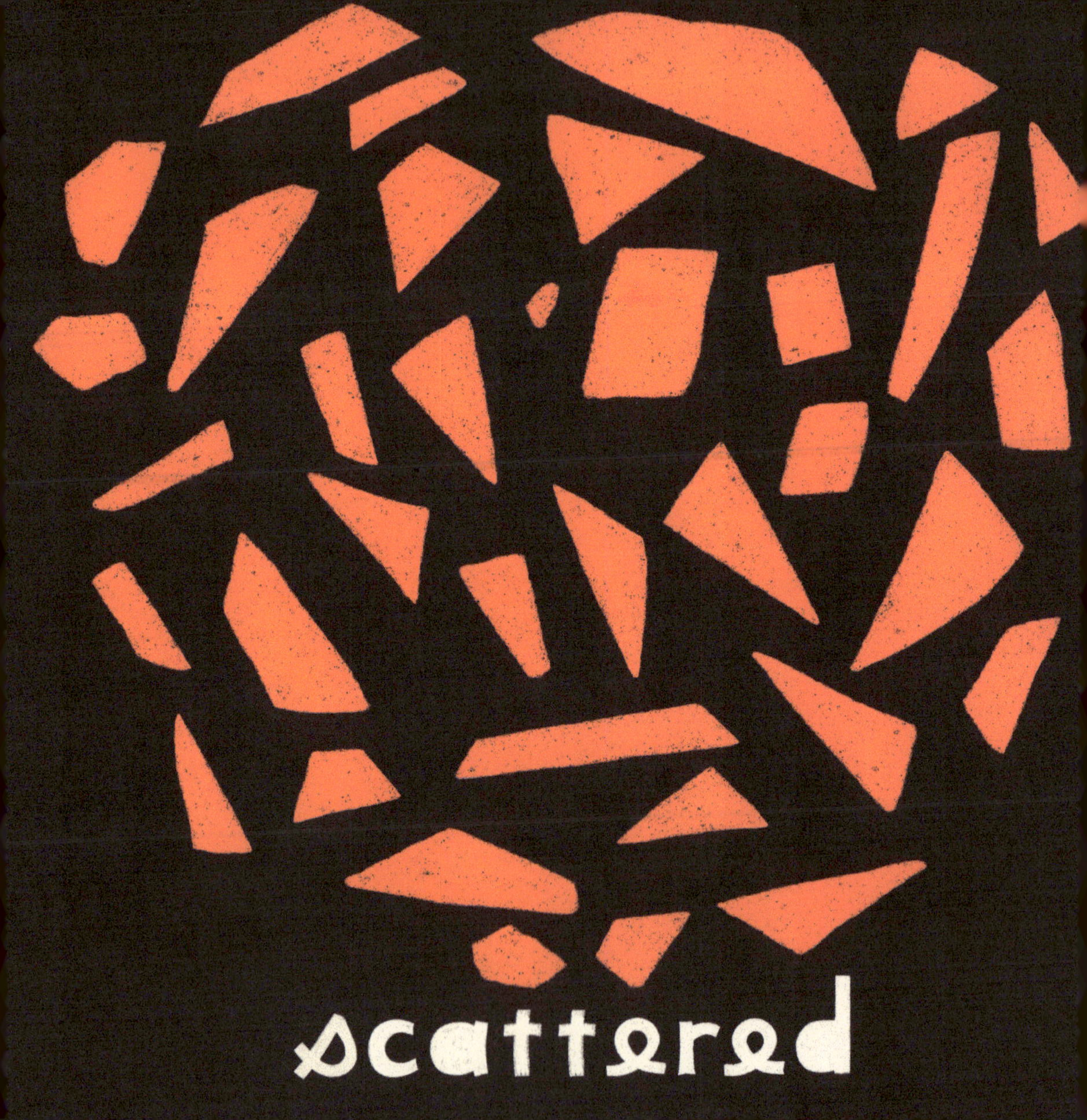
scattered

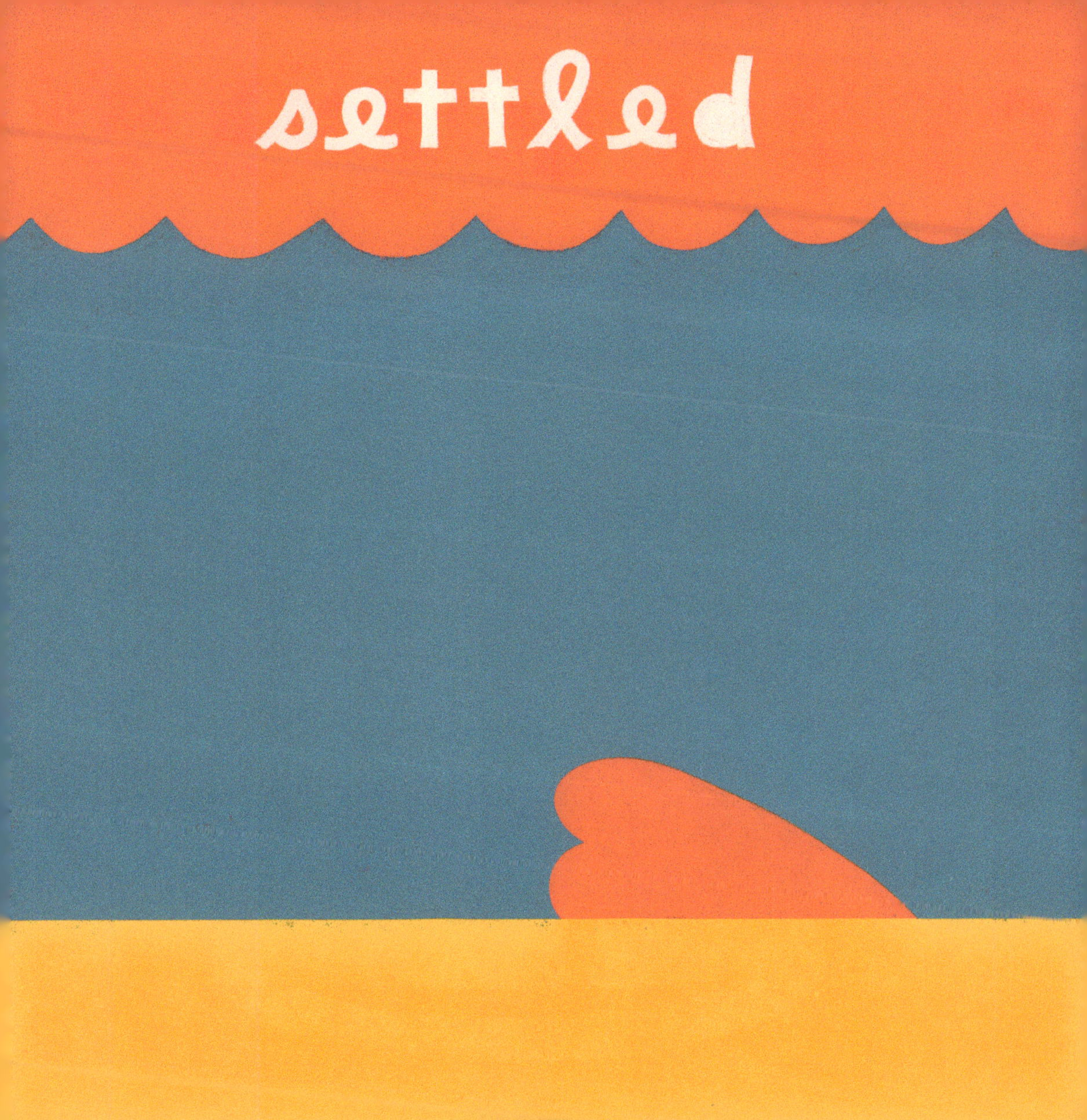
settled

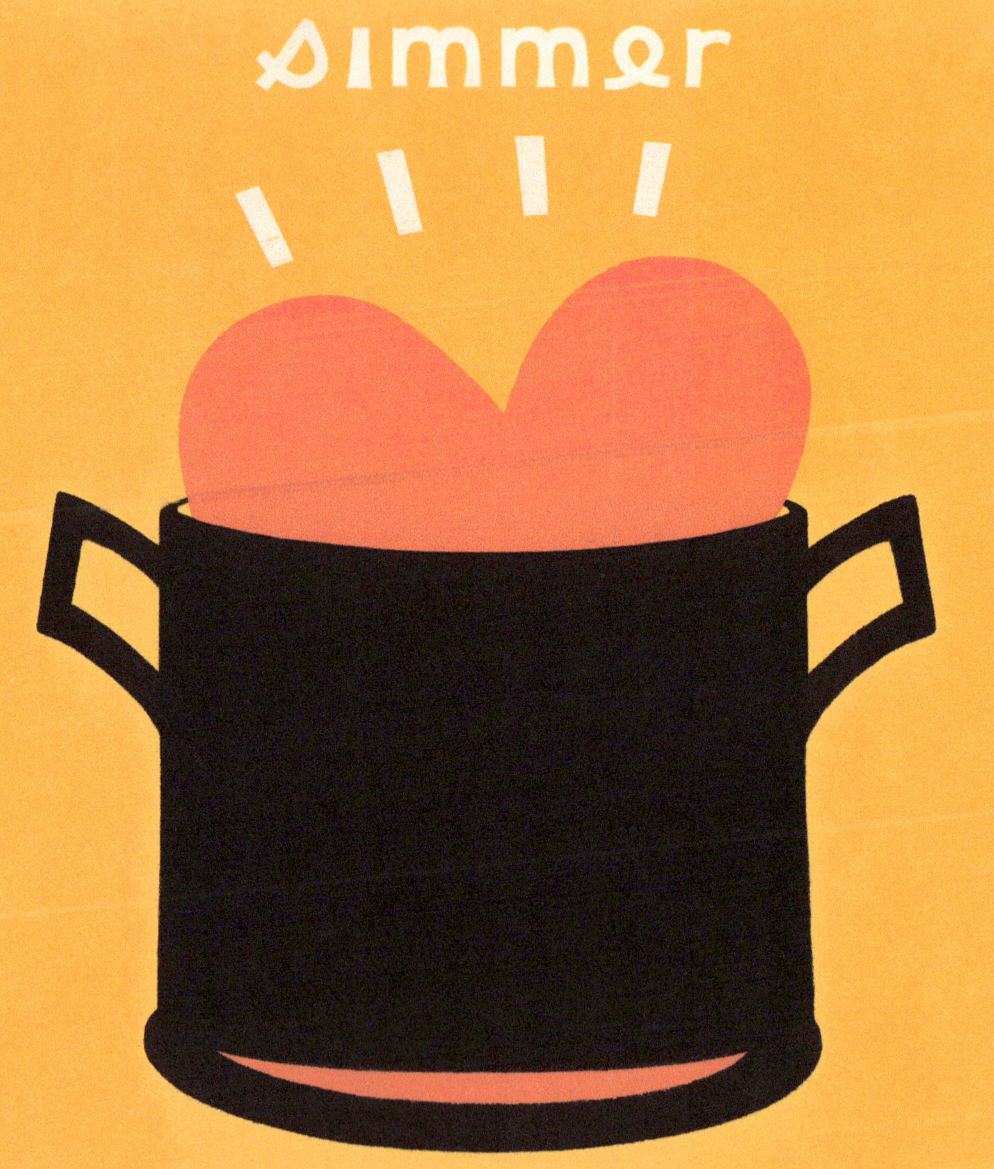
Simmer

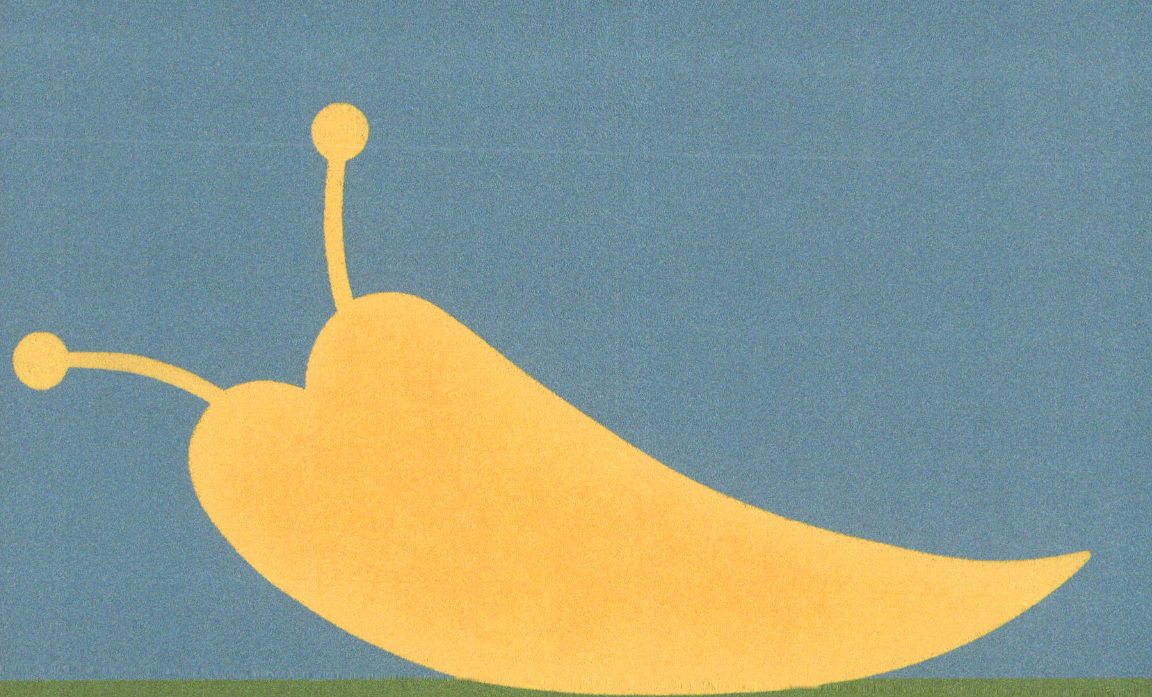
sluggish

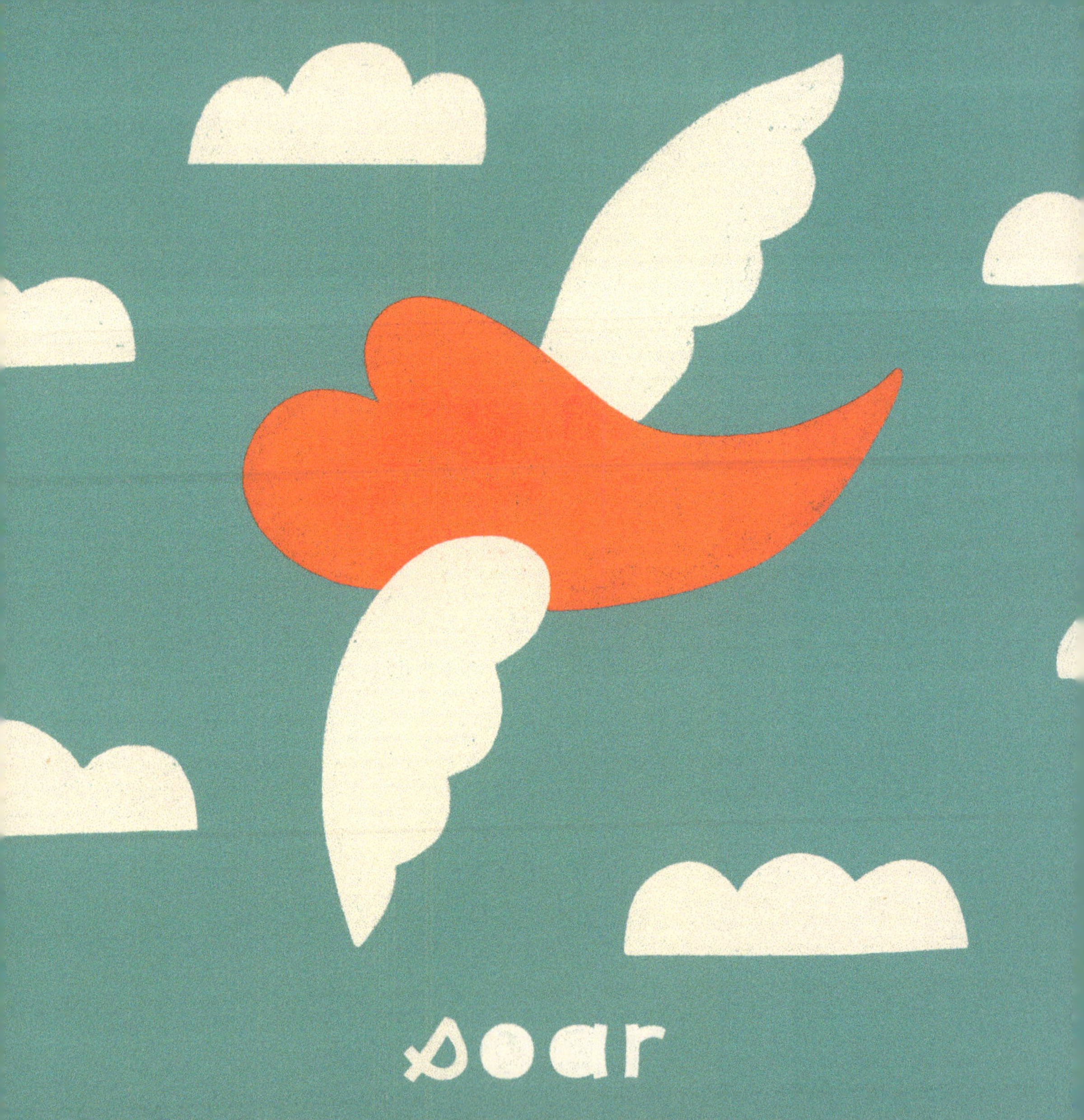
soar

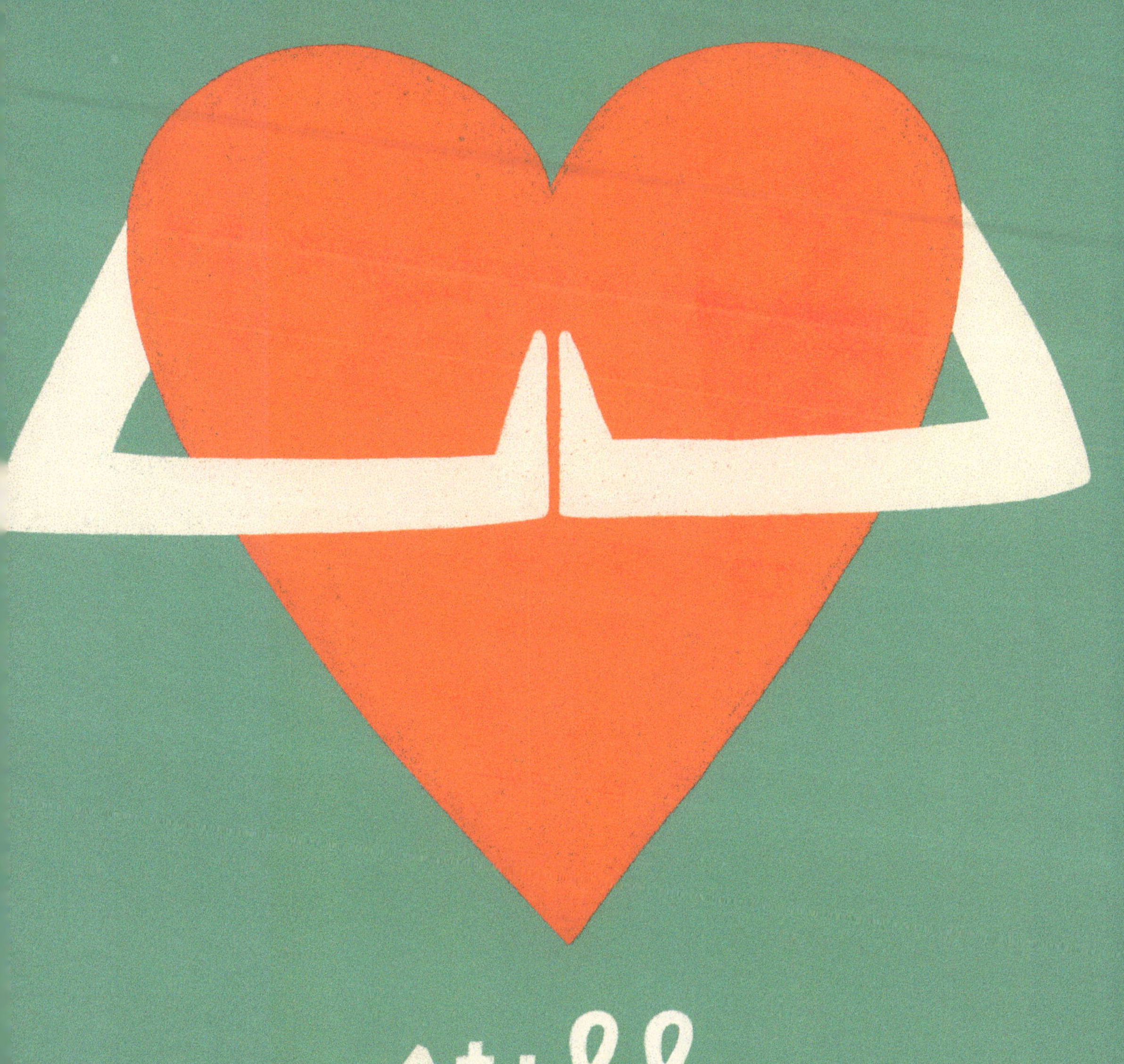

still

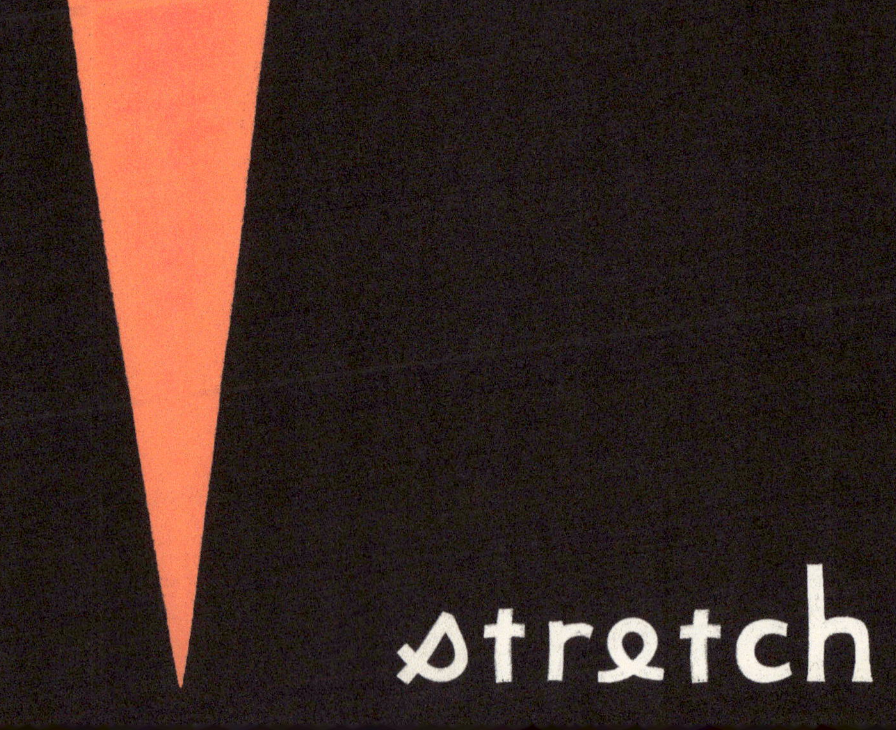
stretch

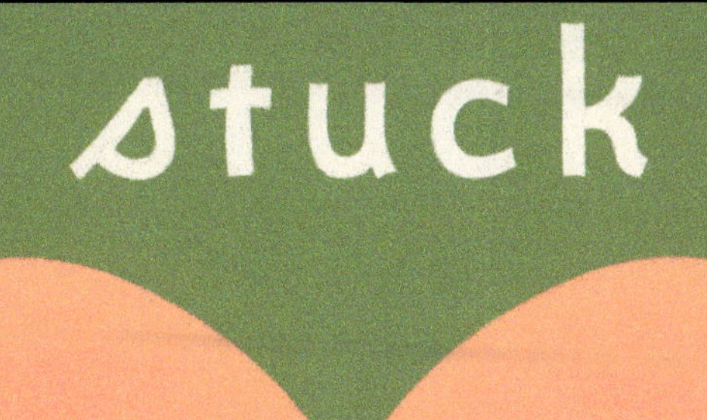
stuck

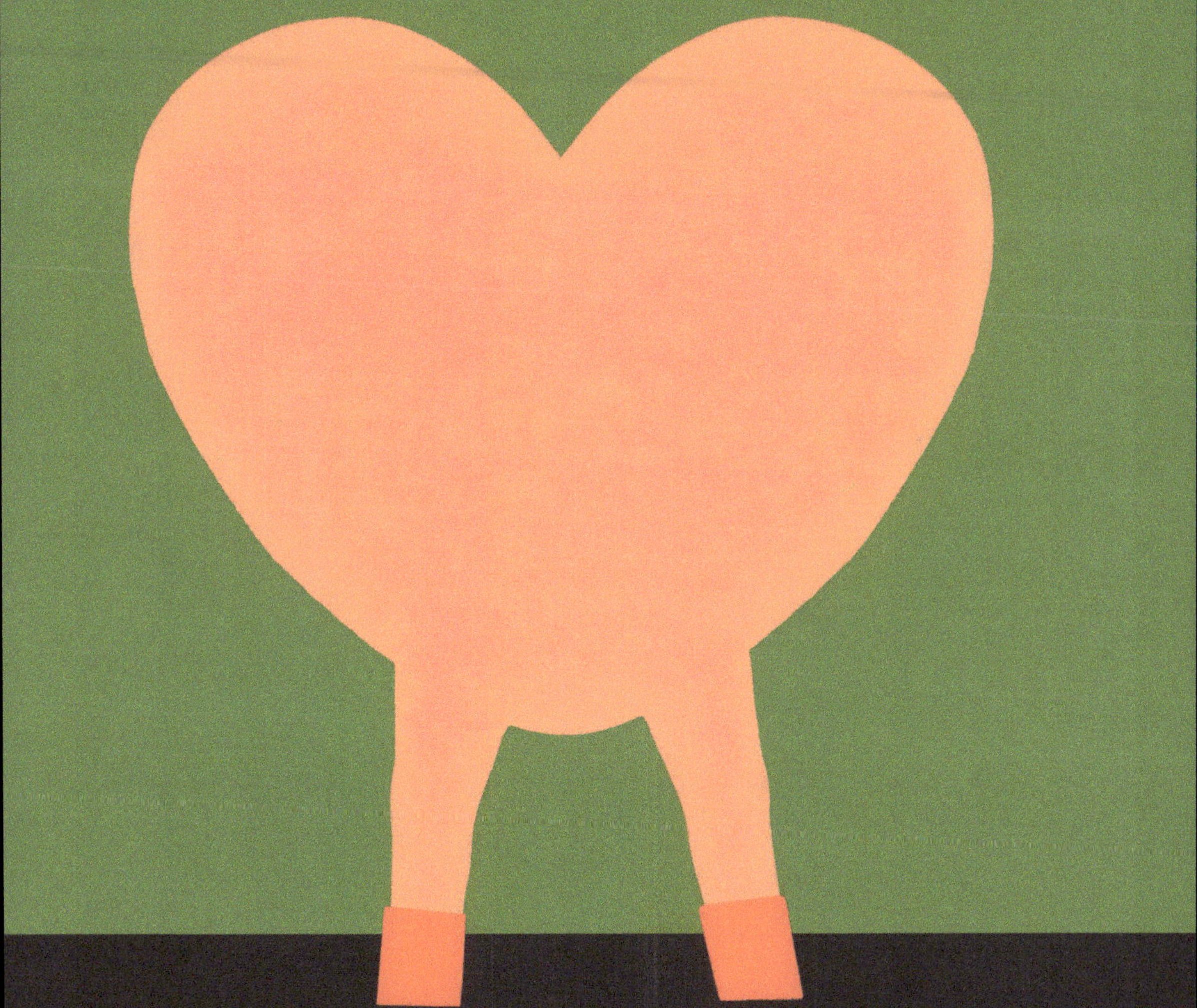

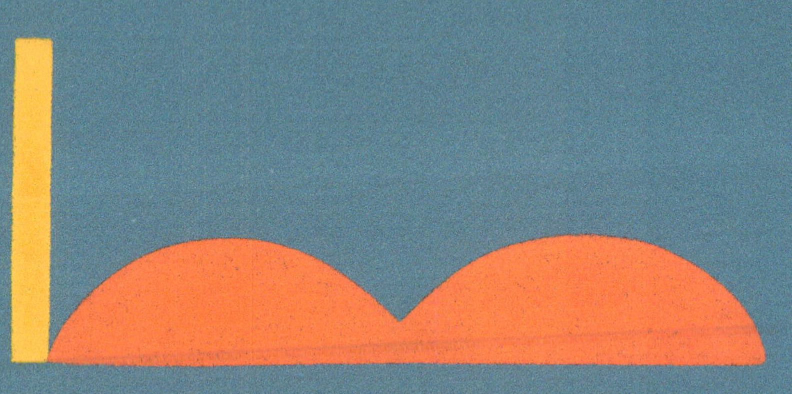

submerged

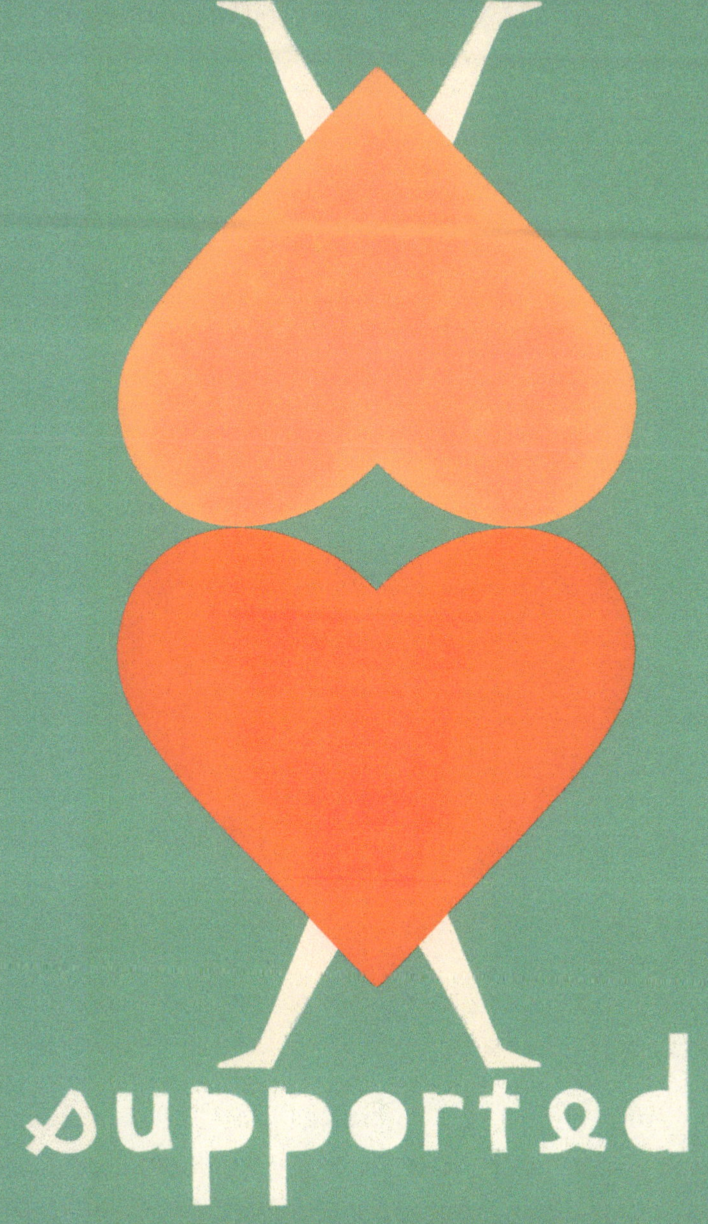
supported

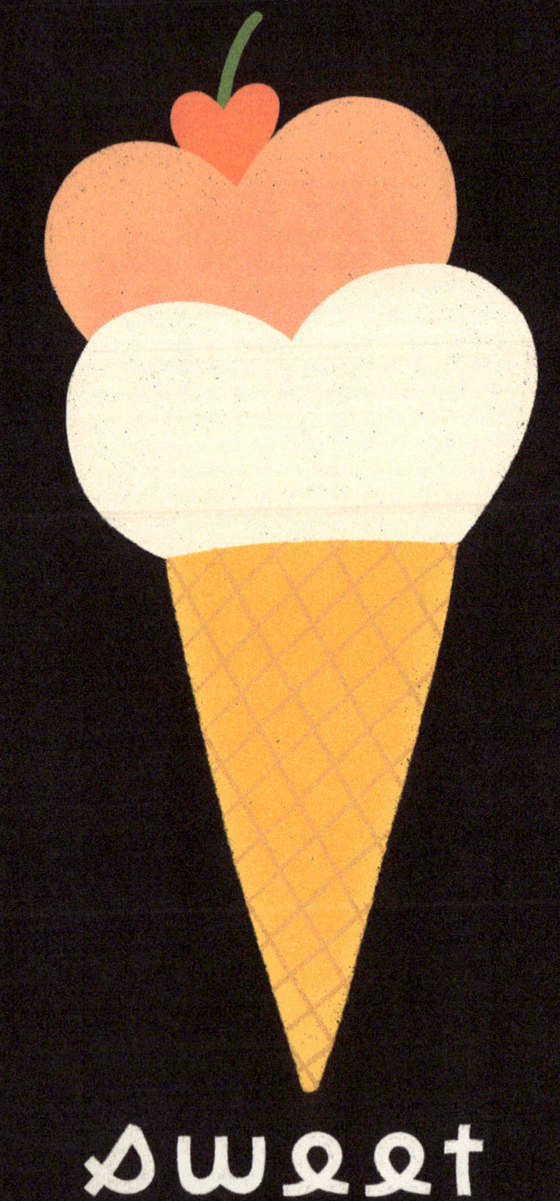

sweet

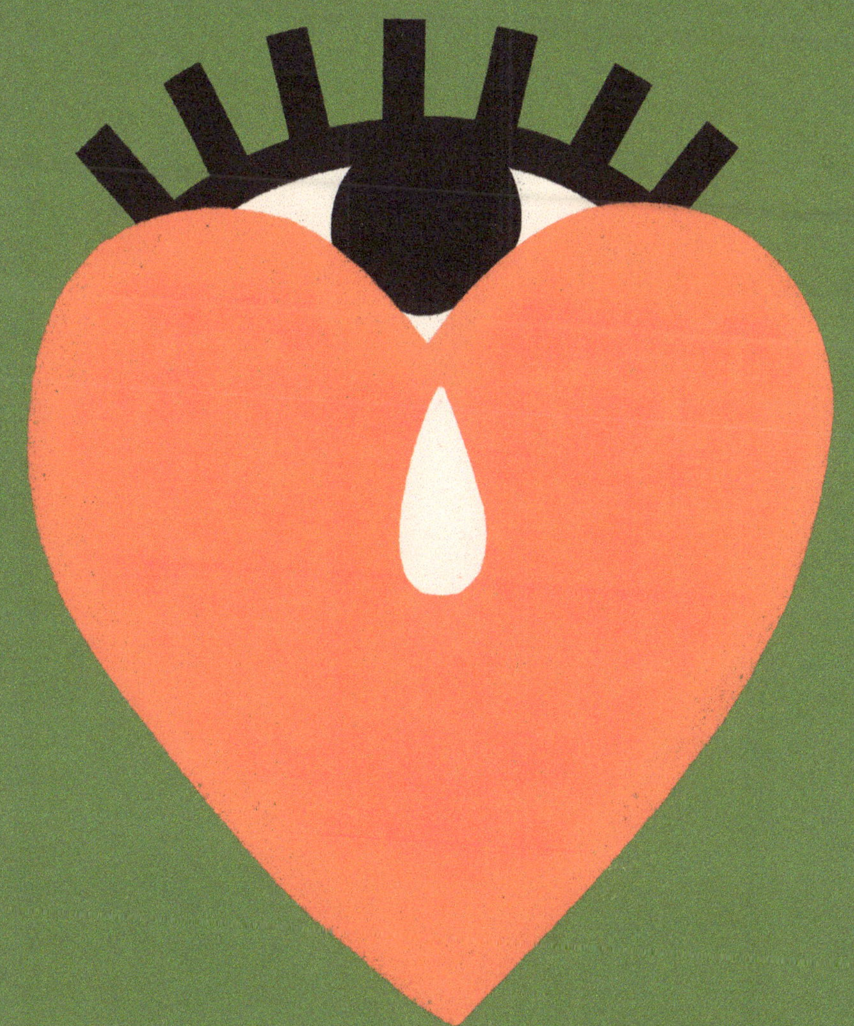

teary

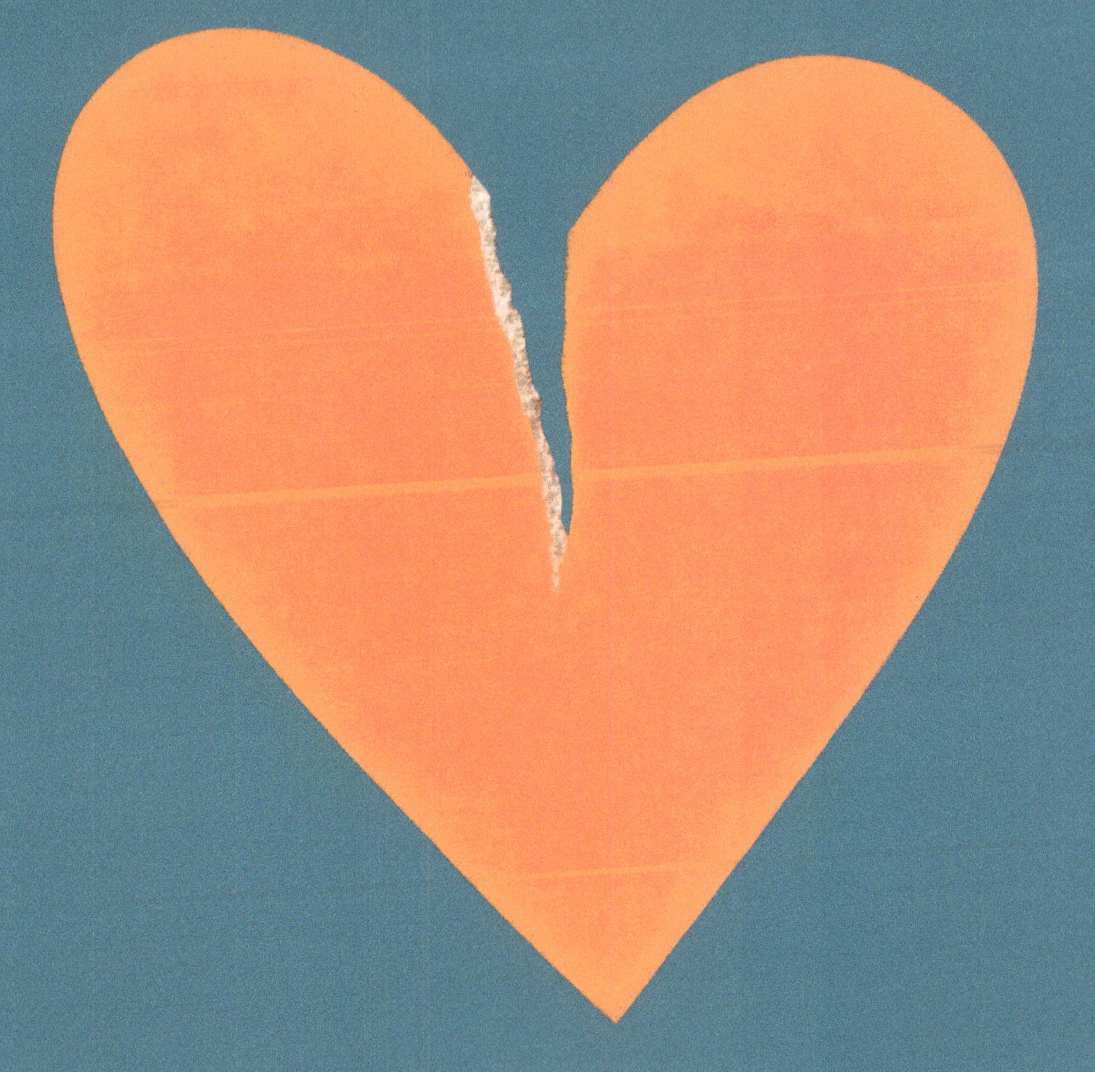
torn

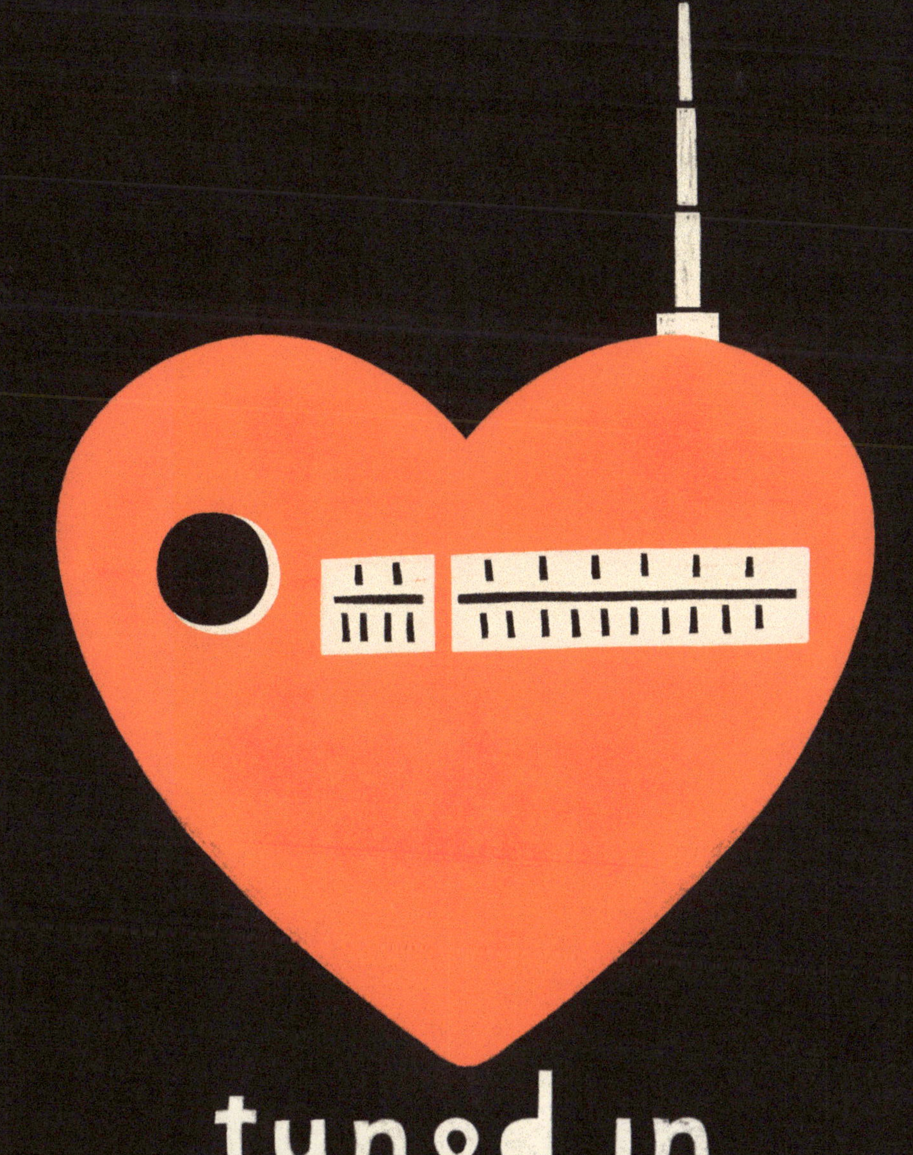
tuned in

uncertain

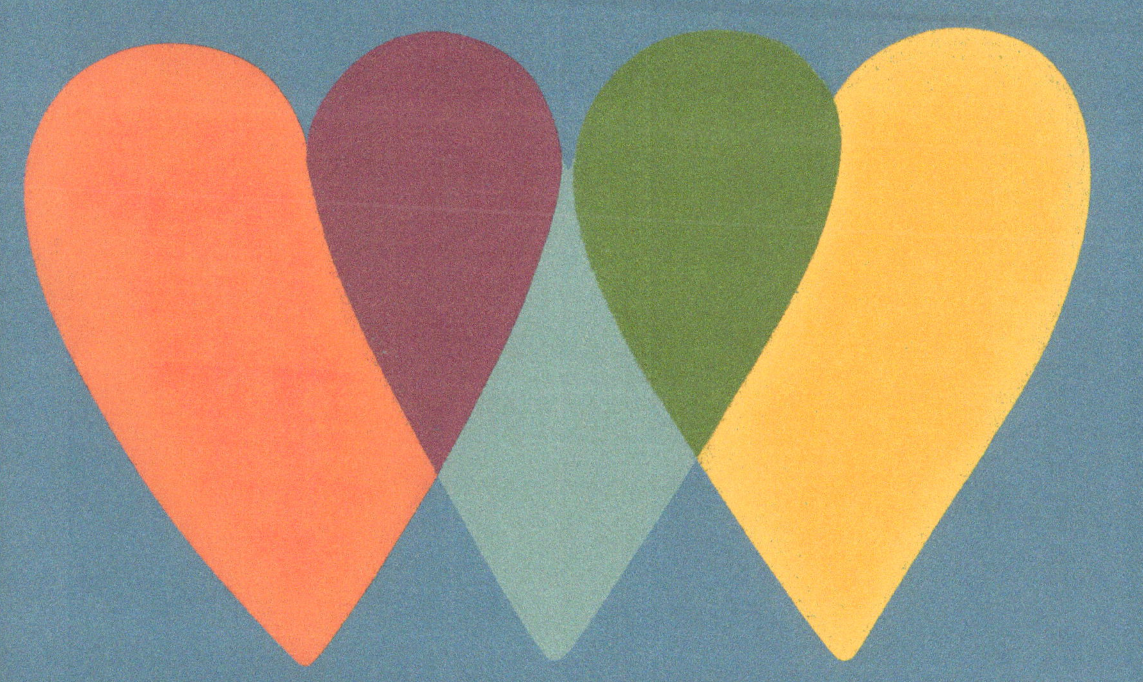

united

unlock

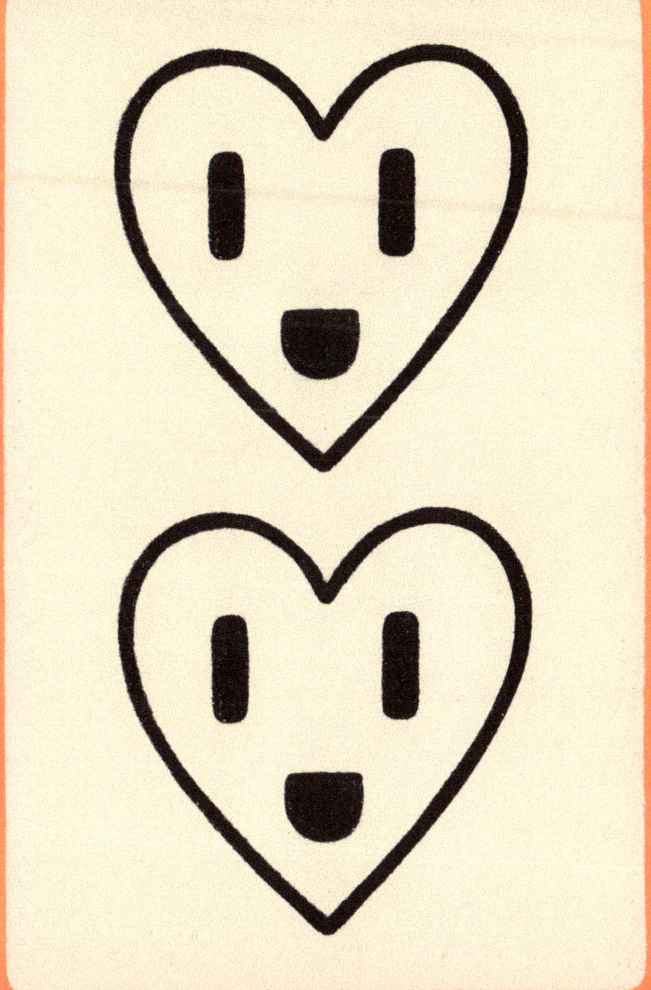

unplug

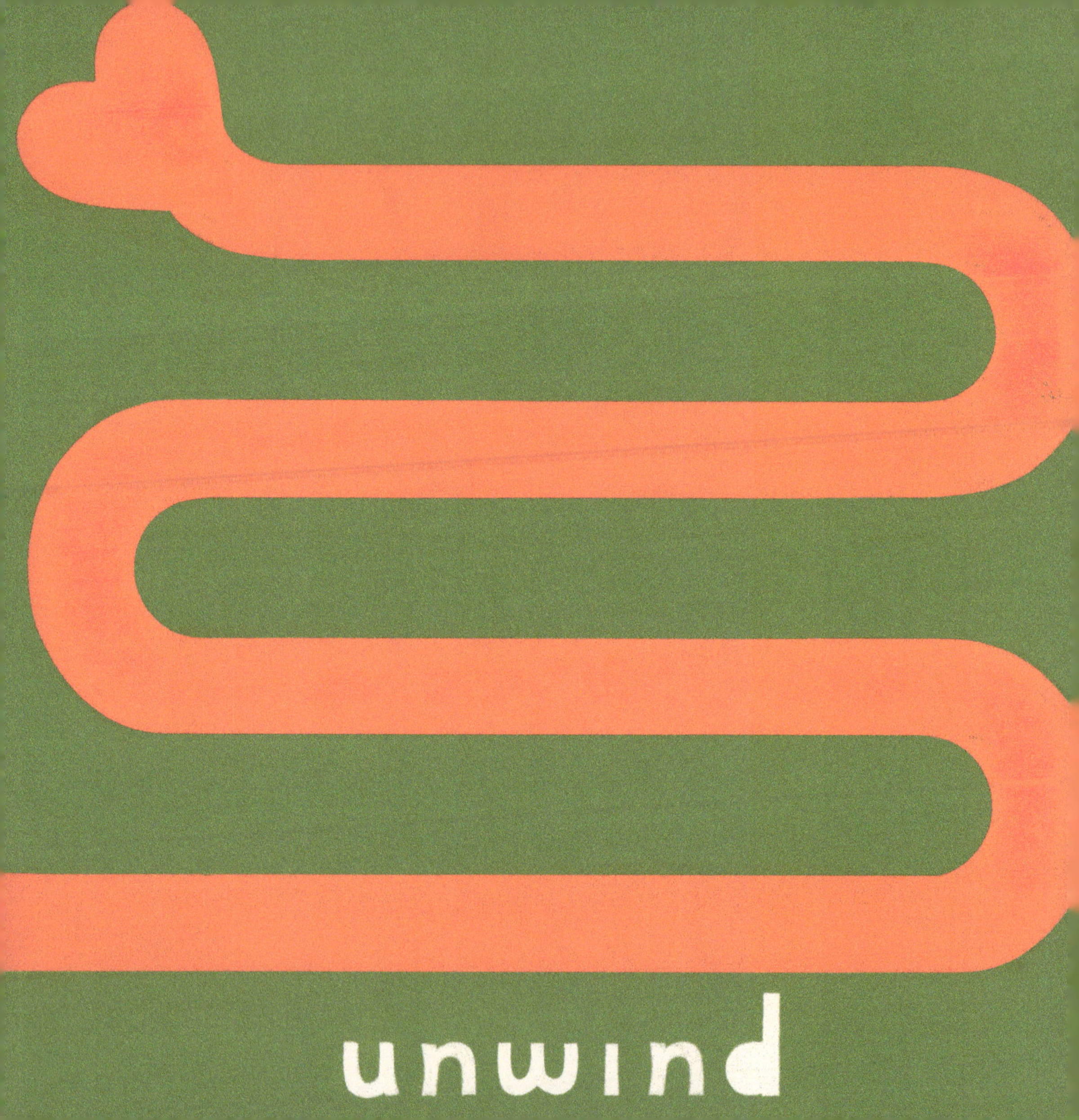

unwind

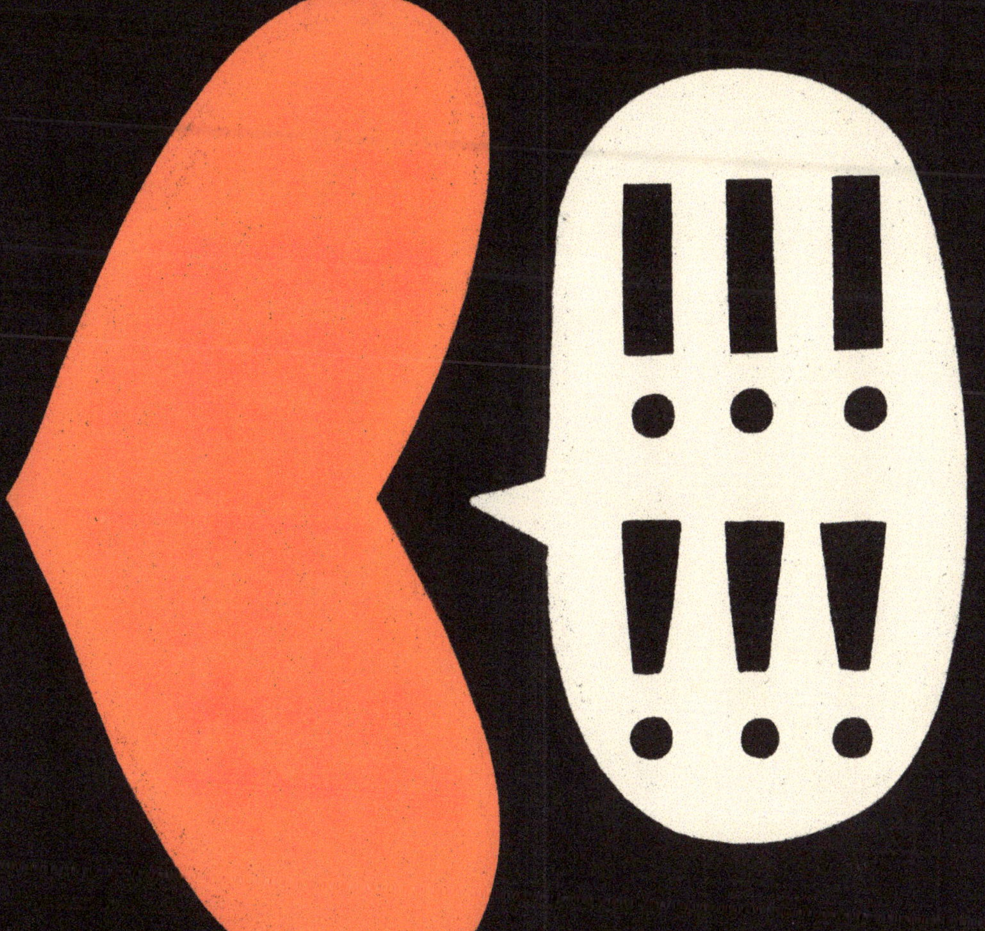

vocal

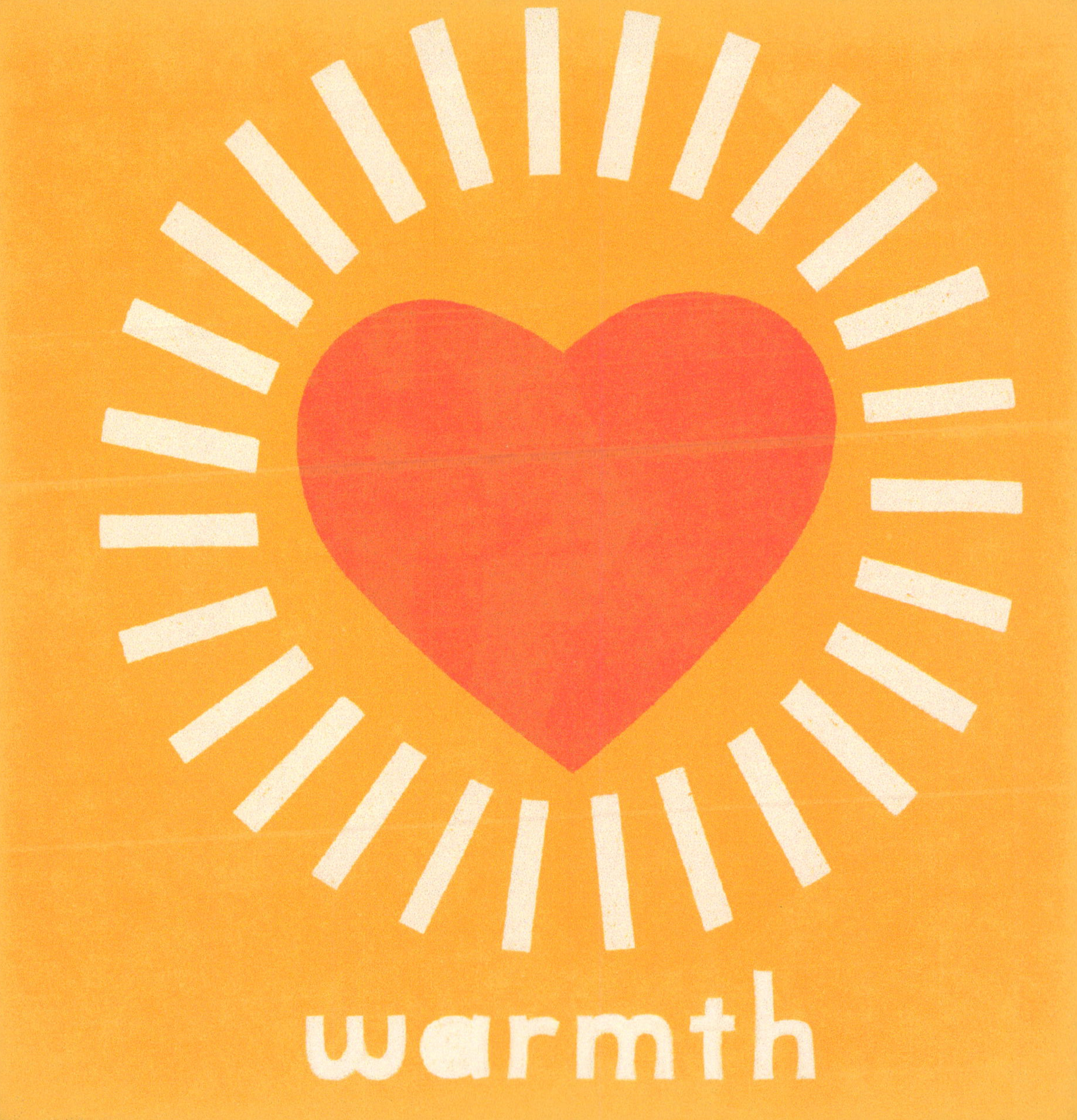

warmth

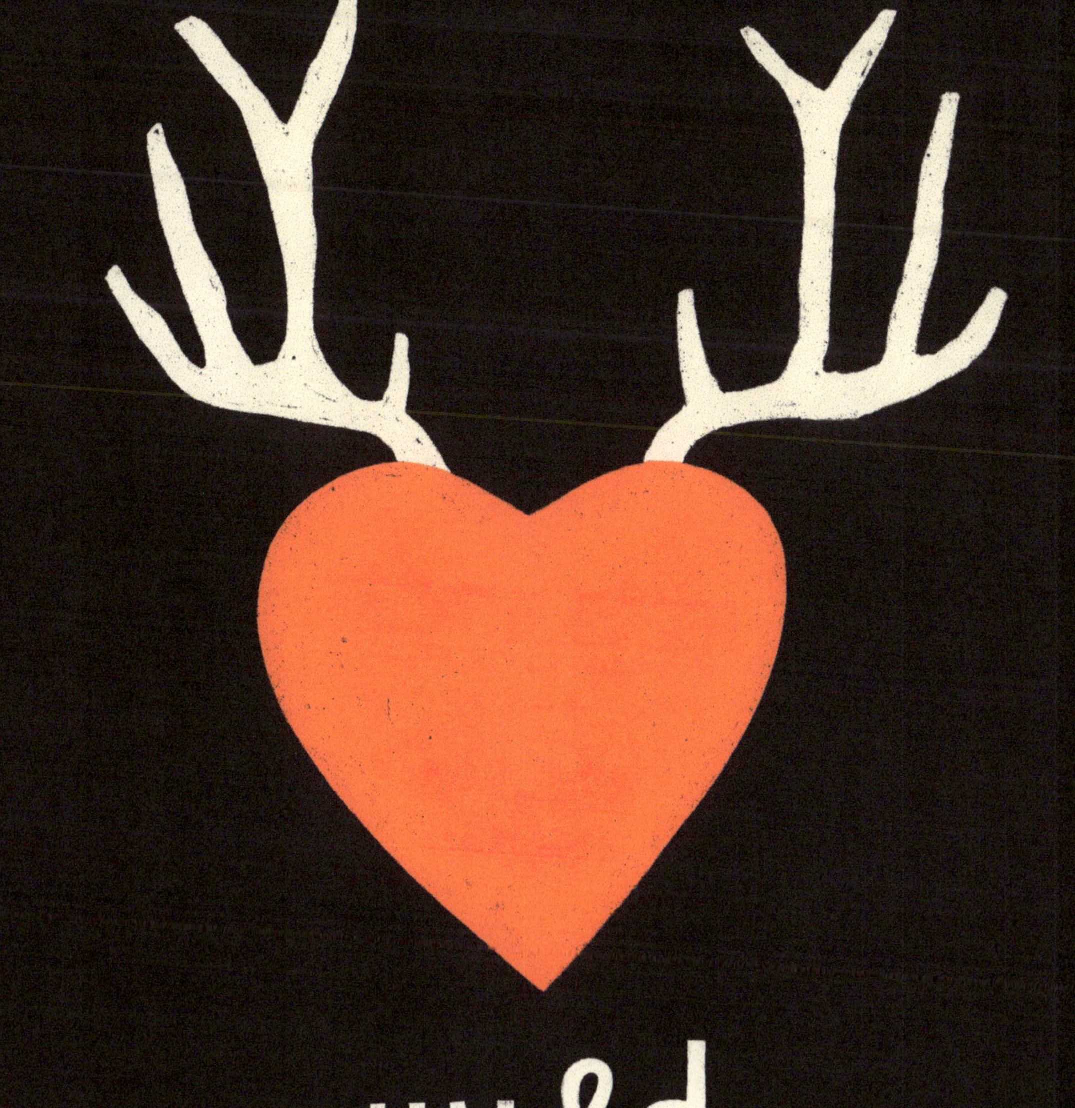

wild

That's not all… come join the 100 Hearts movement!

Do you like being creative, wish you could be more creative, or would like some tips about how to start and keep up a creative practice of your own? If so, then I'd like to invite you to visit the 100 Hearts website (https://www.karenabend.com/100-hearts) where you can sign up for a free 100 Hearts Video Workshop. In the workshop you'll get a tour of the original sketchbooks that inspired the artwork for this book as well as an instructional section where I guide you through my process so that you can work alongside me and create a heart of your very own. A FAQ page is also available that outlines the process and answers common questions about how to get started. It's fun, easy and anyone can do it, so I hope that you'll join me for some heart-to-heart creative time.

Heartfelt gratitude

There are numerous people who directly or indirectly inspired the creation of 100 Hearts. First, the idea for creating something everyday for 100 days was inspired by The 100 Day Project, a creativity challenge I learned about through Instagram that was hosted by Elle Luna. Next, I would like to thank all of the artists who participated in the Sketchbook Revival Online Workshop I hosted and organized for the first time in 2018. A few of the speakers' sessions had a direct influence on my development of 100 Hearts, and I would like to thank them individually: Shelly Klammer, Kiala Givehand, and Anne Leuk. I would also like to express gratitude to the community of creativity lovers from all across the globe who signed up for the workshop and became part of the inspiring Sketchbook Revival community that helps keep all of us going with our practices. Additional thanks go out to Amber Kueileimailani Bonnici for empowering me to create the first Sketchbook Revival Online Workshop and to Elizabeth Foley for her invaluable support. Finally, I would like to thank my friends and family who have supported me with their encouragement and positivity. Nicola and Emilio, especially, who open and touch my heart every day with the love and laughter they bring into my life, and to Jeff for always being there with curiosity, humor and insight.

About the artist

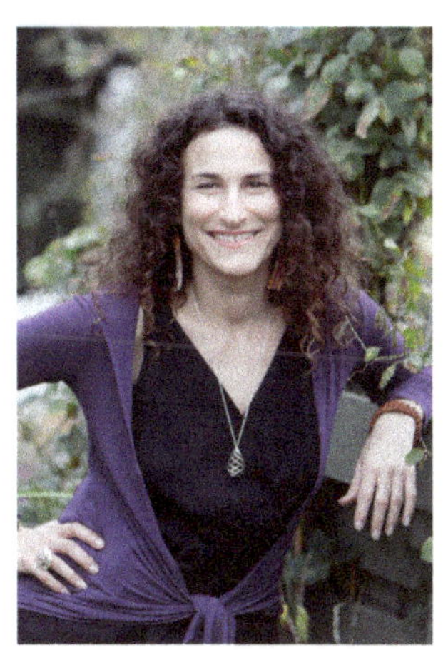

Karen Abend is a licensed artist living in Sicily. She loves to draw, paint, collage, design and illustrate. One of her greatest joys is immersing herself in the creative process and channeling that energy in service of a collaborative project. Some of her favorite projects include designing greeting cards, creating prints and products with her artwork, illustrating a book, and organizing and hosting the online workshop Sketchbook Revival, an exploration of daily creativity in community.

Art and adventure have always been a part of Karen's life. As a child growing up in Los Angeles, some of her happiest times were spent creating with her stash of art supplies and traveling with her family near and far. When it was time to decide on a career, Karen's desire to be immersed in museums, art and art history lead her to the field of art conservation. As an art conservator, her adventures continued, and she worked in museums in New York City and on excavations in Italy, Turkey and Greece.

After moving to Sicily, Karen rediscovered her creative roots and now considers herself extremely fortunate because she gets to spend her days creating art for licensing, personal projects, and always for her own well-being, learning and growth. Since hosting and organizing the first Sketchbook Revival Workshop, Karen has been cultivating her passion for daily creativity and is thrilled to be able to share it with a vibrant online community of fellow creativity lovers. Through Sketchbook Revival she has also discovered how deeply rewarding it is to be able to offer her support to others in developing and maintaining creative practices of their own.

To find out more about Karen you can visit her website www.karenabend.com, follow along on Instagram https://www.instagram.com/karenabend/, or join the Sketchbook Revival Facebook Group https://www.facebook.com/groups/SketchbookRevival/